Waging the War Within

Waging the War Within
A Marine's Memoir of Vietnam and PTSD

TIM FORTNER *with*
ELIZABETH RIDLEY

Foreword by Peter J. Berman, Ph.D., ABPP

McFarland & Company, Inc., Publishers
Jefferson, North Carolina

ISBN (print) 978-1-4766-8068-2
ISBN (ebook) 978-1-4766-4004-4

LIBRARY OF CONGRESS AND BRITISH LIBRARY
CATALOGUING DATA ARE AVAILABLE

Library of Congress Control Number 2020012673

© 2020 Tim Fortner and Elizabeth Ridley. All rights reserved

No part of this book may be reproduced or transmitted in any form or by any means, electronic or mechanical, including photocopying or recording, or by any information storage and retrieval system, without permission in writing from the publisher.

On the cover: *inset*, the author and his lifelong friend Rusty, at LZ Argonne, Quang Tri Province, Vietnam, 1969; *background* troops getting off helicopter in new LZ during Operation Lancaster II (Tim Fortner Collection, Vietnam Center and Archive, Texas Tech University)

Printed in the United States of America

McFarland & Company, Inc., Publishers
Box 611, Jefferson, North Carolina 28640
www.mcfarlandpub.com

To our men and women who have served in the Armed Forces
of the United States of America, past and present.
And to those who have made the ultimate sacrifice
in their service to our country.

"A journey of a thousand miles begins with a single step."
—*Laozi*

Table of Contents

Acknowledgments — ix
Author's Note — x
Foreword by Peter J. Berman, Ph.D., ABPP — 1
Prologue: Happy Birthday, Tim! — 5

1. Surfing, Sex and Justice — 7
2. Journalism, Sex Ed and Extra Credit — 12
3. Mom Dropping F-Bombs? — 16
4. Two New Recruits — 21
5. The Brutal Reality of Boot Camp — 24
6. Getting with the Program — 30
7. "I should have been on that flight" — 36
8. Orders for WestPac — 42
9. Danger Where You Least Expect It — 50
10. Elephant Grass, Alabama Moonshine and a Terrifying Journey to the Twilight Zone — 60
11. Lights and Landings — 65
12. Your Wingman Is Down! — 71
13. The Tiger Bar & Grille — 74
14. Thank You, Anheuser-Busch! — 78
15. Requiem for a Short-Timer — 82
16. Lieutenant Dipshit and the Exploding C-rats — 88
17. The Spoils of War — 93

18. Keeping Watch and a Painful Loss	100
19. Extracting a Recon Team—When Every Second Counts	106
20. Is My Luck About to Run Out?	112
21. Boosting a Jeep from the Military Police	119
22. Seven Lives Gone	125
23. Heading Home	130
24. Sometimes Your Heart Hurts	137
25. Rest in Peace, Rusty	146
26. The Road of No Return	153
27. A Ticking Time Bomb	160
28. Adding Insult to Injury	167
29. A Light at the End of the Tunnel	173
Epilogue: Coming Full Circle	177
Appendix I: Motor Sports History	181
Appendix II: Vintage/Historic Race History Results	183
Appendix III: Statistics from the Vietnam War	187
Appendix IV: HMM 262 Operations, 1968–1969	189
Appendix V: Timothy R. Fortner: Citations and Awards	191
Appendix VI: Timothy R. Fortner: Military Affiliations	192
Glossary	193
Index	197

Acknowledgments

I would especially like to acknowledge the following people who were instrumental in making this book happen.

Peter J. Berman, Ph.D., ABPP—You listened to me. You put into fact what I felt. More than once. You cared and it made a difference. Thank you.

Dr. Calvin Reckord, M.D.—You are a caring man and have my lasting respect.

William Ziegler, Monterey County Veteran's Service Officer—Pushing me was the right thing to do, even though I pushed back. You did your job so very well. My heartfelt thanks.

Dr. Adam Karwatowicz, M.D.—Often, I think about what might have happened with me (and to me) had you not become involved. You care and you are honestly concerned about me (as I know you are with your other patients). Settling me down is something you are able to accomplish—and it certainly has helped. I am a better person because of you. You have my lifelong respect. Thank you.

Dylan Lightfoot and everyone at McFarland & Company, Inc., Publishers—For having faith in my manuscript and making this all happen.

My coauthor, Elizabeth Ridley—Without Liz, my manuscript would have fallen flat on its face. I had an idea and put that idea into words. But they were just words. Liz made it all work. She stayed with the project (that became "our project") for more than five years. Liz pushed for more from me, and even though I disagreed with some of what she was proposing, in the end, she was right.

Dr. Chris Townsend—thank you for introducing me to Liz several years ago and recommending we write this book together. Without you, this book might never have happened.

Author's Note

Waging the War Within: A Marine's Memoir of Vietnam and PTSD is the true story of Tim Fortner's life, and, in particular, his experiences serving as a Marine during the war in Vietnam. Some of the names in the book have been changed to protect individuals' privacy.

Foreword by Peter J. Berman, Ph.D., ABPP

It is with great honor, respect, and privilege that I am writing the foreword to Mr. Fortner's enlightening, painful, and sobering journey from a teenager to a soldier in the United States Marine Corps and his frustrating attempts to seek treatment for his Post-Traumatic Stress Disorder (PTSD). I did not serve in the military, and, ironically, I was attending school in Washington, D.C., from 1964 to 1974 and I witnessed the anti-war movement firsthand. I will always remember the sight of the Vietnam war protesters coming face to face with the rifle-toting National Guard troops and the protesters inserting flowers into the barrels of the rifles that the troops were carrying.

After moving to California, I was employed by the Palo Alto Veterans Administration Health Care System as a clinical psychologist for approximately 30 years. After working on both inpatient and outpatient psychiatric units, I retired from the Veterans Administration (VA) and I worked in the Compensation and Pension (C&P) division of the VA. This is where veterans with medical and psychiatric problems would come to be evaluated so that they could establish their service connection and be awarded monthly financial compensation.

Over the 11 years that I worked in Compensation and Pension, I estimate that I evaluated more than 10,000 veterans with a variety of psychiatric diagnoses. The majority of veterans were male, had served in Vietnam, and had a diagnosis of Post-Traumatic Stress Disorder. Their daily functioning was severely impaired by their mental illness and many of them were socially isolated, unemployed, experiencing problems with intimacy, having severe problems with poor sleep and nightmares, and struggling with substance abuse. My mission at Compensation and Pension was to carefully listen to each soldier's complete and painful story and to review supporting documents from both the VA and from the veteran. I attempted, as best as possible, to be an advocate for the veterans because they were often unable to request the services that they were entitled to. It was often difficult for the veterans to discuss their situations and to even admit to having significant problems functioning on a daily basis. It was extremely problematic and frustrating for me to sit and listen to veteran after veteran describe the horrors of war to which they were exposed and not be able to give them a magic pill to alleviate their pain and suffering. It was shocking to hear a veteran describe landing at the Oakland airport after returning from Vietnam and having to stop in the restroom to change out of his military uniform before heading out of the airport because he might be attacked verbally or physically because he was in the military and had fought in Vietnam.

Although concerned about the veterans, the VA itself has struggled with offering appropriate and effective psychological treatment for its patients. Veterans have always had a love/hate relationship with the VA. The monthly financial compensation is always appreciated, although at times part or all of it is squandered on drugs and/or alcohol in an attempt to self-medicate. Some veterans have a difficult time trusting the VA and they view it as an extension of the system that is out to get them, so they avoid any type of medical or psychiatric treatment.

Post-Traumatic Stress Disorder can result from exposure to any traumatic experience, either in the military or in civilian life. Individuals respond differently to trauma and their symptoms can be very different even if they were exposed to the same event. Depending on the individual, it is often problematic for even the treating professional to recognize symptoms of PTSD so that an appropriate diagnosis can be made and a treatment plan instituted.

PTSD continues to be a major problem in our society and the number of untreated people with PTSD unfortunately continues to increase. Veterans make up a high percentage of the homeless who live on the streets disturbed and forlorn, and they often succumb to suicide. Major strides have been made in the treatment of PTSD both on the inpatient and outpatient basis and with the use of appropriate psychotropic medications. People need to be able to recognize and to admit to having psychological problems and be willing to accept treatment.

Please prepare yourself for a bittersweet and inspiring journey of Mr. Fortner's exposure to the atrocities of the Vietnam war, his witnessing death and destruction, and fearing for his life as you read his very well-written *Waging the War Within*. The author will expose you to events behind the scenes of engaging in combat and being subjected to mortal danger in Vietnam and dealing with the dysfunctional military that one had no idea ever occurred. He will take you on his private journey to hell and back, and you will be pleased that you made the trip with him and you will appreciate your own life maybe just a little bit more. Sit back and join Mr. Fortner on his amazing story about the Vietnam war, its life-changing effects on him, and his attempts to turn his life around.

Thank you for serving your country, Mr. Fortner, and for the many sacrifices that you made while in the military. Welcome home.

Dr. Peter J. Berman is board certified in clinical psychology by the American Board of Professional Psychology (ABPP). He has a master's degree in rehabilitation counseling and a Ph.D. in clinical psychology from George Washington University. He was employed at the Palo Alto Veterans Health Care System (VA) for 31 years and later worked at the Compensation and Pension unit of the VA for 11 years.

Prologue: Happy Birthday, Tim!

"I, Timothy Russell Fortner, do solemnly swear that I will support and defend the Constitution of the United States against all enemies foreign and domestic; that I will bear true faith and allegiance to the same; and that I will obey the orders of the President of the United States and the orders of the officers appointed over me, according to regulations and the Uniform Code of Military Justice. So help me God."

So help me God. With those few, simple words I had, at age 18, officially enlisted in the United States Marine Corps. I was a bright but troubled kid without ambition or direction, and enlisting in the Marines probably saved my life, or at least kept me out of jail. Without the USMC, I'm sure I was facing a judge and jury, or worse, in my not-too-distant future.

In hindsight, I have come to believe that everything that happened afterward—Vietnam, post-war struggles, PTSD and a fight for benefits—actually began on my 13th birthday.

I'm also pretty convinced that Freud could've used me as his poster child.

* * *

May 16, 1961, was my 13th birthday and I could not have been happier. Finally! A teenager at last! I was in history class around 11 a.m. when

Tim Fortner at age 13.

suddenly my uncle Carl from Sacramento entered the classroom, along with Mom and Aunt Peggy. Why were my aunt and uncle in town, and why was Mom with them? She was supposed to be in San Francisco with Dad.

Of course, I thought, excitement rising. *It's my birthday, and we're either going someplace cool, or I'm getting a great gift.* My party was planned for that night, so I just assumed the festivities were starting early. *Life is good!*

I watched as Uncle Carl spoke to my teacher in hushed tones and then came over to me and said solemnly, "Tim, let's go outside."

I got up and followed him. Once we were outside, he said, "You need to be strong. You are going to have to be a man today." And without further preamble he added, "Your dad died last night." Apparently, Dad had had a massive heart attack and passed away.

Only then did I notice that my mother, aunt, and uncle were dressed in black and Mom's eyes were red.

Uncle Carl continued talking as we walked toward his car but I was too numb to focus on anything. I went to hug my mom and she started crying. We held on to each other for a while and finally got in the car and headed to the funeral home.

Happy birthday, Tim. *Happy birthday? Shit!*

1

Surfing, Sex and Justice

After several years of refusing to deal with my father's death and growing into an angry, rebellious, confused young man, I began my freshman year at Soquel High School in Soquel, California. Academically I was lousy, just doing the minimum to get by, but I was an above-average athlete, especially in football, and I enjoyed my newfound interest in girls.

Life was all right, until my mother remarried, to the third of her four husbands. My mother had had a difficult life. Diagnosed with manic depression, Mom married her first husband right after high school. He was a U.S. Army corporal, a tank commander in World War II who was killed in action and posthumously awarded a Purple Heart. My father, Clyde Russell Fortner, was her second husband, until he died in 1961 at the age of 49. Her third husband, whom she married my freshman year, was a wealthy and well-respected doctor in Santa Cruz.

Unfortunately, he was also a pompous ass. She wanted him to be a father figure to me, giving me "the Talk" and explaining the mysteries of life. He let me know that he was a prominent man who didn't have a lot of spare time but would make time whenever I needed to talk "man to man."

After they married, we moved into his house and I transferred to Santa Cruz High School. Santa Cruz in the mid–1960s was the place to be. Surf City, USA. Coconut Grove. The Boardwalk. Beach Street. The girls. Most of all, the girls.

As a 140-pound sophomore, I played football on the lightweight team. I had a very good year football-wise and scored several touchdowns. It was a much better year girl-wise—I scored some touchdowns there, too. But I struggled academically. I couldn't fathom how all that boring bookwork would benefit me later on. I did what I needed to get by, but nothing more.

As my grades fell, I got more grief from my mother and from teachers and counselors. This set off a downward spiral—the worse I did in school, the more I disliked it. But as long as my grades were good enough to keep me playing football, I didn't care about anything else.

Soon, I started cutting school in the mornings to go surf at Steamer Lane

Tim's photograph for the Santa Cruz High School football program, 1964.

or Cowells Beach. I would ride my bike to a friend's house, get my board and wetsuit I kept stashed there, and surf the morning away. Then I'd show up for 3rd or 4th period at school and finish out the day. I got away with this for several weeks, until the school office compared the excuse notes from my "mother" (alias me) with some of her original notes and realized the notes were forged.

Shit!

They busted me and I got my first suspension, for three days. I was supposed to use those days to catch up on my homework. Of course I did no such thing.

1. Surfing, Sex and Justice

Mom was a mover and shaker on the Santa Cruz social scene and had something going every day of the week: a fashion show, luncheon, civic group, or some other BS. That left me home alone, able to hop on my bike and go surf. When I returned to school after my suspension, the teachers asked for the work I was supposed to have done. I told them I hadn't done it. This resulted in study hall detention to catch up. I couldn't dodge that, so I focused on producing just enough to get by and continued bullshitting everybody.

Amazingly, this method saw me through freshman, sophomore, and junior years. I got my driver's license and whined until Mom bought me a car. Then things really became fun.

Having a car opened up lots of opportunities—especially with girls. Santa Cruz was a pretty loose town and getting laid (even at that age) wasn't hard. And if you had a car, it was even easier. Now, not only was I surfing in the morning, I was with a girl in the afternoons, evenings, and weekends. In fact, I think I set new records for sexcapades in the back of a Chevy.

I had one or two steady girls, but that pretty much ruined any extra-curricular activities, so I generally stayed away from steadies. Coupled with that, I still hung around with my best friend from Soquel High, Rusty. Rusty was a chick magnet! He could charm the panties off just about any girl, and most of the time he did just that. He was a big guy, a fantastic football player, had a great smile, and had a gift for gab that endeared him to people. When Rusty and I were together, we were unbeatable.

The summer before my senior year, I'd fixed up the Chevy and it became the car to beat in Santa Cruz. The weekend drags up the coast highway generally went my way and I even made a little money.

We also did a little street racing, 1960s-style. How it worked was you would pull up to a stoplight and peel out with the guy next to you—pretty simple. Except that you won by not only beating the other guy off the line but by getting off the gas last, meaning there was a bit of a game of chicken involved. In the 50 or so street races I took part in, I only lost four outright, and one of those because I missed a speed shift. Other than that, I had a pretty good record. All this succeeded in giving me a bad rap as someone who was reckless, dangerous, or worse.

Unfortunately, my past sins, lousy academic record, and history of cutting class attracted the attention of the Santa Cruz police and the truant officer, Sgt. Vernon, along with the wrath of my high school principal, Mr. Burr.

Burr was a stern disciplinarian and didn't take crap from anyone. I was on his shit list and should have stayed beneath his radar—but I didn't. My next stunt pretty much put me on ice; I just didn't realize it at the time. In fact, several things happened that year that put me on my path to the Marines.

It began when I was suspended for cutting class to go surfing. I probably could have gotten away with cutting class alone. The surfing would have been harder to explain, but I think I could have skated that. I might have gotten off easy ... except for how I finally got caught.

Sgt. Vernon had been targeting me for a while. He would hide out between cars and behind buildings, follow me at night, and so on. He actually ticketed me for "exhibition of speed" in front of Santa Cruz High School (guilty). I blasted off an occasional smoky burnout in front of the school and he would wait to pop me. He was one persistent cop and he didn't like me at all! In fact, he made me his personal project.

When Vernon got word I wasn't at school one day, he headed straight for the beach and found me (along with most of the senior class) surfing at the river mouth. It was about 9 a.m., the surf was great, and we were having a good time. Vernon got on a bullhorn and ordered everybody off the beach and back to school. Everybody obeyed except two guys: me and Rusty.

This decision proved unwise.

People paddled to the beach and scattered. Within 10 minutes, the beach was deserted except for Vernon. He yelled at me and Rusty to come in, so we paddled to the south side of the river mouth and toward the beach; Vernon was on the north side. We managed to evade him long enough to ditch our boards, run like hell, and hop into my car, laughing like crazy. But the police were one step ahead of us, and we didn't get very far before police cars had us blocked on all sides. I watched in the rearview mirror as Sgt. Vernon stopped behind me and exited his car.

Shit! We are really fucked now.

Back in 1965, the local cops could get away with just about anything, and you didn't have to be officially charged to get a talking-to from the police. Vernon and his buddies pulled Rusty and me out of the car, cuffed us, and slapped us around pretty good. Vernon kept asking me if I thought what we did was funny and I told him yes, I thought it was pretty funny.

Slap! Slap! Slap!

It wasn't funny after that.

While this justice was being meted out by the police, a Santa Cruz County sheriff's car pulled up and out hopped Sheriff Mike Armstrong, who happened to be Rusty's uncle.

Great!

Even better, Mike was also a family friend and knew me pretty well. Mike walked past Rusty, slapped him upside the head and continued on to me. Now, Mike Armstrong was a big man, maybe 6'4" and about 250 pounds of solid muscle. He walked over, lifted me up off the ground by my wetsuit, and knocked the shit out of me!

"Tim, you are a fuck-up! I don't like fuck-ups," he screamed in my face.

"We're all tired of your shit. Your mother, the school, the SCPD. Clean up your fucking act, or the next time I have to deal with you, you are going to jail. Understand?"

The simple answer was "Yes, sir!" He dropped me back onto my feet, backhanded me alongside my head, turned, and headed back to his car. On the way, he grabbed Rusty by the handcuffs and dragged him to the car, threw him in the back seat, and sped off.

It got real quiet then. Vernon crossed his arms as he and his boys stood around me, not saying a word. Blood trickled from my nose, my left eye was swelling, my lip was cut, and I was scared to death. Vernon walked up to me and growled, "Okay, smart ass, you get the message?"

Second simple answer: "Yes, sir!"

When I finally saw Rusty about three days later, it looked like Mike had worked him over pretty good. Our parents decided it would be best to keep us apart for a while. I was grounded for a month and the car was taken away. I was given the option of getting my grades up and quit screwing around or going to military school. I knew they weren't kidding.

I decided it was time to pretend I gave a shit and suck it up a little ... but just a little, and only as long as necessary.

2

Journalism, Sex Ed and Extra Credit

The summer between junior and senior year of high school I worked on the Santa Cruz Boardwalk, a rite of passage for kids in Santa Cruz. I worked at the Burger Shack during the day and on the Giant Dipper Roller Coaster in the evenings. The Giant Dipper was a serious chick magnet and Rusty (who was working at the Wild Mouse) and I had more dates than anyone could imagine—sometimes two a night! Life was very good.

But when summer ended and senior year began, everything changed. I wanted to finish high school and get out of Santa Cruz as soon as possible. Over the summer I considered ways to really fuck with my parents and the school. It wasn't that the schoolwork was too difficult—I was just rebellious and did not care. So I decided that senior year I would apply myself, for once.

My classes were freshman English (I was the only student in Santa Cruz High's history to take freshman English all four years of high school, due to flunking the first three times), algebra, world history, PE, mechanical drawing, and journalism. My final grades for senior year were Bs in mechanical drawing and algebra and As in PE, English, and world history. This mystified everyone—Tim the rebel, the fuck-up, with a 3.8 GPA? How could it be?

Senior year I also realized that football would take up a lot of time and I preferred spending that time more productively, preferably with a variety of pretty girls. Also, at 150 pounds, I knew that I risked getting my ass handed to me on the football field.

Goodbye, football.

I earned an A in journalism as well. The class was supposed to be about writing and composition and all that typical shit, but in reality, all we did was put together the school yearbook. Piece of cake. I even became the yearbook's editor-in-chief. Of course, this required a lot of work, some of it after hours.

2. Journalism, Sex Ed and Extra Credit

Tim's senior photograph from *The Cardinal* yearbook, Santa Cruz High School, Santa Cruz, California, 1966 (*The Cardinal*, Santa Cruz High School).

I became interested in a teacher who was at the school in the evenings. She and I began to spend time together and, one thing led to another, and one evening I got up my courage and just flat-out asked her to go out with me.

She got real quiet and I worried I had really fucked up and overstepped the boundaries. She very sweetly explained that the rules of her employment forbid students and teachers fraternizing, and therefore she had to say no. She also added that she thought it was "cute" that I'd asked, and if there were some way to do it without losing her job, she would.

Cute? Hmm.

A few weeks went by and I kept eyeing her. I noticed that, despite what she had said, she would get close to me any time it was possible.

Jeez!

Emboldened by the mixed signals she was sending, I asked if she would consider getting a hotel room in Monterey so we could be together. She said she'd been thinking about it and would let me know. *She'd let me know!* I was on pins and needles, waiting for her decision.

The following weekend we ended up at a motel in Monterey and only ventured out for food. It was fantastic. Here I was, a 17-year-old high school kid screwing a very good-looking teacher!

Life was good!

We had a good thing going and a firm agreement to keep this whole deal secret. It lasted about four months as we pretty much balled our way through most of the hotels in Santa Cruz County and beyond. We even managed a quickie in a class storage room during school hours! She taught me wonderful stuff that I didn't even know existed.

Meanwhile school was going well, I was getting better grades and the yearbook looked like it was going to be one of the best the school had ever produced. Orders were up and advance sales were beating expectations. We decided to order an additional 50 yearbooks to make sure there'd be enough to cover any late or last-minute sales.

When the yearbooks finally arrived, I skimmed five off the top and sold them on the side for $15 cash to pre-arranged customers. The normal cost for a book was $25, so this was a good deal for both parties and I made some extra money. I dummied up the sales books and thought I had gotten away with it.

I was wrong.

An inventory of all the orders and receipts showed that five books were missing. It was pretty easy to trace where the yearbooks had gone (even though the evidence was largely circumstantial). I had to repay the money and my A+ in journalism suddenly became an F.

Fortunately, I didn't get expelled.

Sgt. Vernon was notified of my latest fuck-up. Another black mark on my already dismal record, and yet another strike was about to come from a most unexpected source.

One morning after class I stood at my locker, located right next to Mr. Burr's office. The school wanted to keep an eye on me and monitor my attendance.

Suddenly a voice behind me said, "You fucking asshole, you can't talk to me like that!" I turned around and a guy named John Baldwin was standing there, red-faced with balled-up fists. I knew John in passing, but not well. He started screaming at me and took a swing that I was able to dodge.

I asked him what the fuck he was doing and he said, "You told me to pick up your book last year in English. You can't order me around, asshole!"

I had no idea what he was talking about. *Last year? What the fuck?*

He took another swing and I bobbed again. By this time a small crowd had gathered and I suggested to John that we continue this outside.

He ignored that request and swung at me again. He caught me in the shoulder and I hit him fast twice, straight in the nose. Down he went and I leaned over and said, "Let's finish this outside and not in here!" He launched a swing from the floor and missed.

Fuck it!

I smashed his nose. His head was on the linoleum floor and had no place to go to absorb my shot.

Crack!

Blood and snot everywhere and a broken nose. John was screaming and thrashing around on the floor, holding his face. What a mess.

From behind me, a loud voice bellowed, "Into my office! Now!" It was Mr. Burr.

Shit! Now I was really fucked.

2. Journalism, Sex Ed and Extra Credit

All Burr saw was me ruining Baldwin's nose while he lay on the floor, defenseless. He didn't see how it started so he assumed I'd started the fight.

Fuck! Fuck! Fuck!

I went to Burr's office as an ambulance came and hauled Baldwin off to the hospital. Then my mother, Sgt. Vernon, and the vice principal showed up.

There would be no trial, no questions asked. This was a done deal. They all agreed upon a seven-day suspension. The next offense would mean automatic expulsion from the school system.

I tried to explain that I hadn't started the fight but they refused to listen.

This time, the suspension was enforced and my mother hired a housekeeper/jailer to ensure I did my homework and didn't leave the house.

Great.

I served my time under house arrest and returned to school on a probationary basis. One more wrong move and I was out.

About a week after I was back in school, I was called into Burr's office. Already there waiting were Burr, my mother, and John Baldwin (with a black eye and white tape on his smashed nose) and John's mother.

John started by saying, "I'm sorry I started the fight with you."

I responded with silence.

"I was having trouble at home and I shouldn't have taken it out on you," he continued. "I'm sorry."

Silence.

John's mother chimed in. "We're very sorry for the inconvenience and for causing Tim a problem. This was not any fault of his. John is really sorry."

I just stared at them.

Now it was Mr. Burr's turn. "Thank you. We appreciate you and John coming in to shed some light on this matter."

"Well, Tim has a history of getting into trouble. We thought this was just a continuation," my mother added.

Thanks, Mom! Still I said nothing.

Now Sgt. Vernon added his two cents. "Tim, it was only reasonable to assume that you had started the fight."

I walked out of the office without saying a word. And that was the end of it. No "Sorry," no "We rushed to judgment," no "We'll take the suspension off your record." Nothing. This just made me more bitter and angry, determined to leave that hellhole as soon as possible.

3

Mom Dropping F-Bombs?

As senior year continued, I tried like hell to stay out of trouble, graduate, and leave town. My grades were good, the girls and the sex were great, but I was ready to be someplace else. I didn't know where, only that it had to be far from home.

I was in my fourth-year freshman English class on a Tuesday in August when two uniformed Santa Cruz police officers came to class and escorted me to Mr. Burr's office. I immediately knew this was going to be bad.

I was running through my mind all the stuff I'd been doing, trying to figure out what they were going to bust me with this time, but I couldn't think of a thing.

In Burr's office I was met with the normal cast of characters including Burr; my mother; Sgt. Vernon; the vice principal; the president of the Santa Cruz City School Board, Mr. Henderson; and a cop I didn't recognize.

While the two uniformed cops stood at the door, Mr. Burr got up and said, "Tim, we've all had enough of your antics. You are a dangerous and disruptive element for Santa Cruz High and for the school system. You have repeatedly been in trouble, with this school and the police. We have given you the benefit of the doubt. I can speak for everyone in this room when I say that we have tried everything to help you."

Then, he dropped the bomb…

"I observed you doing a burnout with your car yesterday morning along the entire length of the street in front of the school. Not only is this dangerous, you could hurt or even kill someone. Sgt. Vernon has previously cited you for this offense. There will be no more warnings. Officer Caulkin from the Santa Cruz police traffic division has written you a citation."

Burr presented me with the citation. Then, he handed down my sentence, reading from the letter in his hand. "By order of Santa Cruz County Schools, the Santa Cruz City School District, and Santa Cruz High School, you are hereby expelled from Santa Cruz High School."

3. Mom Dropping F-Bombs?

Bummer.

The place was dead silent. My mother looked pale, the two uniformed cops smirked, and Burr and Sgt. Vernon looked thrilled.

I didn't say anything. There wasn't much to say.

When we got out of Burr's office, Mom told me to go home and she'd meet me there.

So I walked home (about a mile and a half, uphill) to wait for the hangman or the executioner or whatever was about to befall me.

I was fuming! I hated school, hated the fucking house I was living in, hated everything. I was tired of hearing that I had potential, if I would only "apply" myself. I was tired of everyone telling me what to do and how to act. I wanted out—I just didn't know where or how.

I was utterly and completely lost.

When I got home, my mother was already there and she asked why it took me so long to get back, especially after she had told me to go straight home. She was about as pissed off as I had ever seen her.

Well, I was pissed off too!

Rather than answer directly, I asked how long it took the high school's kangaroo court to reach their verdict. I asked where the evidence was, other than Burr's accusations. She said she thought the accusations were probably enough, given my past history (hard to argue there). There was some substance to what she was saying, much as I hated to admit it. I told her that I was definitely a fuck-up, I was really sorry, and I would try to do better. "It's a little late for that," she replied.

Then I poured out all my pent-up frustrations, saying that I hated school, I hated Santa Cruz, I hated her, I hated her dumb-ass husband, I hated everybody. I said that if I could figure out a way to leave, I would.

I also told her that while most of the time the accusations against me were true, sometimes they weren't. This was one of those times. I reminded her of the John Baldwin fight and that I hadn't done anything wrong. There were also other incidents in which I'd been unfairly implicated.

Then I told her, "The reason it took me so long to get home is because I walked. I don't have my car."

She looked totally confused.

I went over to my desk and pulled out two receipts. One was from Surf City Motors in Santa Cruz. The receipt and work order were dated on Monday for a transmission repair to my Chevy. The other was from Rossi Towing showing that I'd had the car towed to the dealership on Saturday night, right after I'd blown up the transmission.

Doing the math, if my car had been in the shop for repairs since Saturday night, it was now Tuesday, and my alleged burnout had occurred on Monday, something didn't add up.

No car, no burnout.

No shit!

I explained this to Mom and told her I didn't give a damn anymore. I said she could sell the fucking car; I didn't care what she did with it. I told her I wouldn't go back to school. Ever. I called Rusty to come pick me up and then I split.

I stayed at Rusty's that night, figuring out what to do next. I was in some deep shit, some of it my fault, some not, but most of it *was* my own doing, I had to admit. I was having trouble with my mother and her husband. The school principal had made it his personal mission to destroy me. The Santa Cruz police had me on their A list. I was way past rebellious, had a bad attitude and a worse temper, hated school, and was about as arrogant as it gets. Totally out of control and heading for disaster.

It was time for a change.

My only real option after high school was going to the local junior college to buy some time. I figured it would be a short stay but maybe long enough to get a job or find direction. Despite my anger and attitude, I was actually concerned about where I might end up.

When I returned home the next day, Mom grabbed me and told me to get in her car. Off we went to the high school and straight to Burr's office. Mom said nothing more, and I just figured they had found a way to send me to San Quentin. This time only Burr and Mr. Morgan, the superintendent, were in Burr's office.

We were soon joined by a guy in a suit whom I'd never seen before. My mother introduced him. "Mr. Burr, Mr. Morgan, this is my lawyer, Mr. Black. I want you to listen very carefully. I have asked Mr. Black to join us to inform you and the school district that we are going to sue the fucking shit out of you!"

(*Those were her exact words. She actually dropped the F-bomb! Holy shit!*)

"You will reinstate my son immediately, clear up his record, and don't ever fuck with him again! Do you understand?"

Burr's short answer was "Yes, Mrs. Vance, I understand completely."

To the superintendent she said, "Mr. Morgan, if there is one more problem with Mr. Burr and my son, I will sue you and this fucking school out of existence. I will have this school razed and I will build a park on the property! Do you understand?"

Mr. Morgan's short answer was "Yes, ma'am, I understand. Thank you for your understanding in this matter."

"All I understand is that you have been gunning for my son, and I'm tired of it. Remember what I've said! Now, good day." And then we left.

But not before I stopped at Burr's office door, walked back to his desk, pulled the ticket out of my wallet, said, "Hey, do me a favor and take care of this, will ya? Thanks," and dropped the traffic ticket on his desk.

My mother was waiting for me outside. I walked up to her, smiling, but I was shocked when she reared back, smacked the shit out of me, wound up, and smacked me again. "Get in the goddamn car and shut up!"

She chewed me out the whole way home. "You have a problem and you're not even trying to fix it," she seethed. "You are a troublemaker with no respect for anybody but yourself. You are very lucky—you just dodged a big bullet. When you are in the right, I will defend you, but when you are not, I am not going to bail you out anymore. This is it! Straighten up and once you graduate, either get a job, go to college, or get out—I don't care; I just want you gone. I've had it. Do you understand?"

Everything she said was true. I was a pretty big fuck-up, a spoiled rich kid, arrogant, extremely rebellious. I had no case to argue, so I told her I understood. At least I got to hear my mom use the F-word a bunch of times on those guys. Pretty cool. But what *was* I going to do? Not just for the rest of high school, but for the rest of my life?

* * *

I spent the summer after senior year working at the Boardwalk and having a great time, but when summer was up, I still had no clue what I wanted to do. I applied for a couple of lame jobs but they didn't really appeal to me. It was 1966 and Vietnam was in full swing; I was classified 1-A for the draft. This was not good. I thought maybe I could wrangle some sort of student deferment by going to junior college. Rusty was going to Cabrillo Junior College in Aptos, so I enrolled too, signing up for Introductory Mathematics 1, Physical Education 1, American History, Astronomy, and Study Hall 1. These classes were not difficult, to put it mildly. PE involved playing volleyball in the gym, astronomy was held in a darkened room with stars on the ceiling, allowing me time to sleep, and I basically just blew off history and math. In other words, I had lots of free time on my hands.

Study hall was held in the student cafeteria and there were always people coming and going. There were also lots of girls, and this became what you might call a "target-rich environment." I was able to hustle chicks and get dates at a great rate. I learned absolutely nothing but got laid quite a bit. I would start organizing the football party on Monday or Tuesday each week, and by game night, a bunch of people were lined up at somebody's apartment for a pre-game and then a post-game party. While football season was on, we partied like there was no tomorrow. I even sold my textbooks to buy wine for the parties.

Not surprisingly, eight weeks into my college career, I was flunking every course. My counselor explained that if I withdrew from my classes by 10 weeks into the term, it would not reflect on my transcripts. My counselor also informed me I was 1-A for the draft, and if I stayed at school it was probably too late to pass any of my classes anyway. And, more important to me, football season was almost over and the parties were going to end.

Shit. Time to bail out.

The worst part was having to explain to my mom that I had dropped out of school. Of course she went nuts! It was either get a job or get out—preferably both.

It was crunch time.

I told Rusty I was thinking about going into the Navy and he suggested the Air Force instead, because his brother was in the Air Force. I didn't much give a shit where I went; I just wanted out. I knew that if I did nothing, pretty soon I would get a draft notice and then I was going to really be fucked! The only thing I knew for certain was that I did not want to be drafted into the Army and end up in the hellhole of Vietnam.

So I decided it was time for a pre-emptive strike. Little did I know, my brilliant plan would plunge me directly into the heart of darkness raging halfway across the world.

4

Two New Recruits

Having decided that the best way to get the hell out of town was enlisting in the military, I drove to the recruiting center in Salinas. The building had four separate offices, one each for the Air Force, Navy, Army, and Marines. So I walked into the Air Force office and confidently told the guy I was ready to enlist. He looked at me like I was crazy—they had reached their quota and there was a waiting list. Guys who were likely to be drafted into the Army were trying to join the Navy or Air Force to avoid being sent to Vietnam.

Oh shit! But I filled out the forms anyway and the guy told me to check back in a week. This was November and I checked back every week, and every week I got the same story: I was on the waiting list. At about number 10,000.

So on my next visit to the recruitment center, I walked next door to the Navy recruiter and told the guy I was ready to enlist. He gave me the same story as the Air Force guy, put me on a waiting list, and told me to come back next week.

Around this time, Rusty decided that he, too, was not really cut out for college and dropped out. His parents, like mine, went ape shit! Rusty was given an ultimatum similar to mine, so he accompanied me on my next visit to the recruiting offices in Salinas.

Rusty got the same story I had gotten and was put on the same waiting lists by both the Air Force and Navy. Our weekly trips continued into December. Sometime around mid–December, I asked the Navy recruiter where I was on the list and he told me I was now at about 5000. The Air Force recruiter had worse news and this really pissed me off. This whole deal was fucking nuts. Here we were, two bright, healthy, young American men, trying to enlist in the military, and we were constantly being told they were full. What a load of crap.

I was so pissed off that as I walked out of the Air Force recruiting office, I turned into the next office, which just happened to be the Marine Corps recruiter. Once inside I found a crusty old master sergeant sitting behind a desk with a burned-out stub of a cigar in his mouth and his hands folded on his desk. Like the smart ass I was, I said to him, "Hey, pal, your two buddies down the hall have waiting lists. Do you have a waiting list too?" I will never forget his response. He didn't even blink as he looked me squarely in the eye and said, "You got your toothbrush, sonny?"

Without a moment's hesitation, I asked him for the papers and signed my name. The whole process took about five minutes.

Rusty stood at the door, open-mouthed. He couldn't believe what I'd just done. *I* couldn't believe what I'd just done! Thinking quickly, I looked at the recruiter and asked, "Do you guys have a 'buddy system' or something?" The recruiter answered that the Marine Corps did indeed, and would my friend be interested in joining too? The Marine Corps' buddy system guaranteed that Rusty and I could stay together through boot camp and infantry training. Rusty was turning green and looking for a place to run and I asked what he was going to do. For a few seconds, he was speechless. He finally muttered that the Marines were the toughest, meanest bunch, their training was brutal, it would be really scary, blah, blah, blah.

End result: The United States Marine Corps signed on two new recruits that day.

Semper Fi!

I was ready to leave immediately but Rusty wanted to wait until after Christmas. I went along with that. It was already December and a few days more wouldn't make much difference.

During the drive back to Santa Cruz, I was gloating, thinking that my family would be sorry now. *I really showed them! Boy, are they gonna feel bad. Fuck you all!!!*

When I got home that night, my entire family was there, my mother, her asshole husband, and my sister. I said I had an important announcement to make. It went something like this: "You guys have given me a hard time for a while now and I'm tired of it. I enlisted in the Marine Corps today and am outta here on December 28 for the next four years!" Then I stood back, folded my arms and smirked, letting them absorb my words.

The room was deadly quiet as they all stared at me, wide-eyed. I really showed them! Then my mother let out a "Whoop!" and started yelling and laughing and saying, "Great!" and "I'm finally going to get some peace!" and my sister was yelling shit like "Good!" and "Finally!" and the prominent Santa Cruz physician asshole said, "It's about time you showed some balls, Tim. Any chance you can leave earlier?"

Wow! I really showed 'em, didn't I?

* * *

Going to Marine Corps boot camp was like going to another planet—foreign and very scary. It was everything everybody had warned us about and

4. Two New Recruits

more. All the books and movies about boot camp only scratched the surface. This was terror and pure hell.

But it began innocently enough with the induction physical at Oakland. Which I flunked.

Great.

My urine sample showed a high albumen count and that bounced me from the physical.

At that point, I could have had a rethink and dodged military service entirely. But instead I waited a week, retook the test, and passed. The induction physical was just like a normal physical, and you had to be pretty messed up to fail. The guys who'd enlisted didn't want to flunk and they all seemed healthy and in good shape. But the guys taking their physicals because they were drafted and *did not* want to be there were a trip. They had every malady and disease known to man. For example, they'd limp and then fall down on the floor. Some of them had tics and would shake uncontrollably. There was one guy who pulled out a big knife and threatened everybody. One guy actually pissed on one of the doctors. These guys had all sorts of stories about their health and why they really shouldn't get drafted. Pretty amusing, overall.

Rusty and I were notified by mail that we'd passed our physicals and were instructed to go to the Oakland induction center to take the oath. So we did, and then the nice people at the induction center gave us bus tickets to the Oakland airport and plane tickets from Oakland to San Diego. Everything was pleasant and friendly and everyone at the induction center was helpful and courteous. This was going to be easy, I assumed.

Prior to going to the induction center and taking the enlistment oath, Rusty and I both got all our hair cut off. We also packed like we were going on a day trip. We left all our jewelry, watches, and rings at home. We dressed simply in jeans, T-shirts, and tennis shoes. We made sure we were clean-shaven. We removed everything from our wallets except a few dollars and our driver's licenses. We had the clothes on our backs and a change of underwear—that was all.

We'd been warned in advance.

It was December 29, 1966.

And I was 18 years old.

5

The Brutal Reality of Boot Camp

The plane landed at San Diego and about 20 of us got off the flight and went looking for the bus to the base. Along the way we found other guys also looking for the bus. A guy in Marine Corps dress blues was standing at the exit of the baggage claim area with a hand-printed sign that said "Marine Corps Recruit Depot." We headed that way and the guy told us to get our stuff, go outside, and get in line beside one of the blue buses waiting at the curb. Piece of cake, right? This was going to be easy.

Russ and I got in line. We'd agreed earlier not to talk or call attention to ourselves. Other guys were straggling out carrying suitcases and stuff. Some were talking and eating candy, smoking, or drinking sodas. Once most of the guys were outside, the entire world as we knew it came to a sudden and violent end.

Guys in Marine Corps uniforms suddenly appeared and started screaming at us to get on the buses. Because we were in a public area and lots of civilians were milling around the baggage claim, there was no profanity or physical contact—just a lot of yelling. I remember running for a bus door and hearing the civilians snickering and laughing at the spectacle.

Once we were on the bus, a couple of sergeants got on and the bus doors closed. Guys were still talking and trying to get their suitcases under the seats while others were still eating food and drinking sodas.

The buses pulled away and the two sergeants started screaming, "You fucking maggots! You useless pieces of shit! When we get to the base, we're going to beat the fucking shit out of you, you fucking assholes! Now shut the fuck up and keep your eyes to the front!" One of the sergeants walked down the aisle tearing off baseball caps and grabbing and throwing the Cokes and food the guys had been holding. Some of the guys who were talking got punched and slapped around while these two sergeants continued screaming at us.

"Listen up, assholes! We are now entering the United States Marine

5. The Brutal Reality of Boot Camp

(From left) Tim's best friend, Rusty; Tim's mom, Janet; and Tim at boot camp graduation, March 1967.

Corps Recruit Depot! You are going to remember this day for the rest of your lives! You are shit! You are maggots! You are fucking useless! I'll bet some of you are queer! You are *not fucking United States Marines*! You probably won't *ever* be United States Marines! The Marine Corps does not allow pussies! You people are all pussies! You are fucking recruits, and by the end of tonight, some of you will be in the brig and some of you will be at the base hospital! The rest of you sorry fucking assholes will be mine! I am your drill instructor and your worst fucking enemy! I am not your mommy or your daddy! I am your drill instructor and you will address me as such! You will say, 'Yes, drill instructor' or 'No, drill instructor'! Do you assholes understand?"

There were a few "Yeses" and "Yes, sirs," but everybody was so scared nobody said much of anything. So he started screaming, "I can't hear you!" and we said, "Yes, sir." He kept yelling, "I can't hear you!" and we started yelling, *"Yes, sir!"* until he went on another rant.

When the bus pulled into the parking area, the sergeants screamed at us to get out and find a set of yellow footprints painted on the asphalt and stand there. We were ordered to stand in the footprints exactly as they were painted. One sergeant was at the rear pushing people out and one was at the front pulling people out and they were both screaming like crazy. Guys were falling out of the bus and tripping over suitcases and each other, trying to find yellow footprints to stand on. All the while the drill instructors screamed and thumped on guys.

More Marine Corps guys in uniform were waiting for us on the asphalt and they started screaming at us too. They began pushing and shoving guys and making them stand at attention and stand in the yellow footprints, and some guys at the back weren't doing it right and got beat up. Those guys were crying and screaming and they got the shit beat out of them.

The guys in front couldn't see this, but they could hear it. All the Marines in uniform were yelling and slapping people and ordering us to face the front. The guys who were getting beaten started to fight back and then they really got thumped. We could hear their bodies hitting the ground. Ambulances showed up and quickly hauled them away.

Our drill instructor went to the front of the formation and said, "I told you some of you useless maggots were going to the hospital and some of you pussies were going to the brig! Five of your useless fucking friends just left and I can send more! You are useless pukes and you have no rights! We can do anything we want to you and nobody will do anything to us! You are fucked!"

"When I tell you, you will turn to the left. I will say, 'Left face,' and you will all turn left at the same time. Left is that way." He pointed to his left. "If any one of you useless fucking sacks of shit turns any other way but left, the assistant drill instructors will beat the fucking shit out of you. *'Left face!'*" he ordered, and sure as shit, a few guys turned the wrong way.

Thump, thump, thump.

"Now I will say, 'Forward march,' and you will start marching with your left foot first. *Forward march!*" he yelled, and it was a giant mess. Guys were stumbling and running into each other and falling down. The drill instructor finally shook his head and said with disgust, "You people are fucked. You are a herd of idiots. Okay, herd, just follow me and try not to fall down."

We were then led to a building with four doors and ordered to line up in front of the doors. "You maggots will now get your first Marine Corps-issue haircut. If you have a mole on your head, you will point at it and say, 'Mole, sir.' If you don't, your mole will be cut off."

5. The Brutal Reality of Boot Camp

We were rushed through the doors and saw about 20 barber chairs lined up. One guy would get in a chair and within 10 seconds he was as bald as a cue ball and another guy would take his place. It took about two minutes to go through 40 guys. The barbers had the finesse of rock apes and the clippers felt like hedge trimmers bashing your head.

There was blood everywhere.

The guys with long hair (and there were quite a few) got a bunch of shit. The drill instructors asked them if they were queers and sucked cock. They asked one poor guy with really long hair if he was a "pitcher or a catcher." They wanted to know if the recruits were from Texas and if they were "steers or queers." It was ruthless.

We all ended up outside again and were herded to another building. This building had one door, and we were lined up and pushed through it one at a time. Through the door was a huge room with long tables arranged end to end. Once we were inside, a guy yelled at us to line up at the tables. On the tables were cardboard boxes of about 15 square inches. The drill sergeants then ordered us to strip. So we got undressed and were told to put everything on the table.

So here we were, about 40 bald guys standing in a cold room, totally naked.

Nice.

The Marine Corps guys began to inspect our clothes and belongings. Some guys had wallets and keys. Some guys had pocketknives and combs. Other guys had candy. There was all sorts of stuff. One guy had naked pictures of his wife and the drill instructors got a big kick out of passing the pictures around in front of all of us.

A few guys had dope and that was a bad deal. They were arrested on the spot and dragged away, naked and bald. By that time, a few of the guys were so scared that they pissed themselves, and the drill instructors got a kick out of that.

We were told to take our pile of stuff, place it into a box, and write our name and home address on the box. Everything we came here with would be sent away.

With that done, we were herded through another door and a guy measured our height and waist and we went to a line where another guy threw clothes at us. With our arms full of clothing, we were herded into yet another room where we put on the clothing they had given us—green pants, a yellow T-shirt, green socks, and white tennis shoes.

Very sporty.

We were then herded outside and to a group of several Quonset huts with bunks, no sheets or blankets. The drill instructor ordered us to hit the racks.

So passed my first day in the United States Marine Corps. *Tim, what the fuck did you get yourself into this time?* Well, at least it had gotten me away from home.

A few of the guys cried for a while but the rest of us just sucked it up and tried to sleep. It was about 3 a.m.

After what felt like 10 minutes, the drill instructors crashed into the Quonset hut, grabbing guys and throwing them on the floor, screaming for us to get up. They marched us to the head for showers and the toilet. We were given 30 seconds for the shower and 30 seconds for the toilet.

We were also taught to shave, the Marine Corps way. There were about 20 sinks in the shower room, 10 on each side. We all lined up behind a sink, about three deep. The drill instructor grabbed a guy, slapped shaving cream on his face and said, "This is how you will shave. You will do it exactly like I show you. You will take no more than 30 seconds to shave. If you take longer, the next man in line will take your place and you will not be able to rinse off your face. Is that clear?" A chorus of energetic *"Yes, sirs!"* followed. Some of the guys had never shaved in their lives—they had no clue. Others had shaved only with an electric shaver.

The drill instructor grabbed a safety razor and a safety blade dispenser and said, "You will unscrew the bottom and insert a blade in the top like this." And he demonstrated. Then he took an empty razor and turned back to the recruit and said, "You will make one stroke from your right ear to your chin. This is stroke number one. You will then make one stroke from your left ear to your chin. This is stroke number two," and he made two swift passes on the recruit's face. "One, two! You will then make one pass below the first pass on each side, strokes number three and four, and then make four strokes from under your chin to your neck in a fan shape." He proceeded to demonstrate. "Finally," he said, "you will make three short strokes from your nose to your upper lip and three short strokes from your lower lip to your chin. Is that clear?"

This was followed by another rousing chorus of *"Yes, sirs!"*

The first line of guys loaded their razors with blades on the drill instructor's command, slathered shaving cream on their faces, and the instructor said, "One," and the guys at the sinks made their first downward strokes. He then said, "Two," and the next stroke was made.

What followed was a bloodletting of absolutely epic proportions. By the time all the strokes had been counted out, the sinks were awash with blood. The drill instructor then called for the next rank to step forward and take their turn in the massacre. It was absolutely fucking crazy.

From there, leaving a trail of fresh blood, we were herded to the mess hall and told to line up, grab a tray, and walk down the line. There were guys dishing out stuff with big spoons and ladles. If we did not want something we

5. The Brutal Reality of Boot Camp

were told to say, "Sir, no, thank you, sir." The food was actually pretty good, and by the end of training we couldn't get enough. But on that first day, we'd already been up half the night with little sleep. It was still only 5 a.m. And we were scared shitless. Some guys were crying. The food, at that moment, was so unappetizing that most guys took as little as possible. We were then herded to a table and told to remain standing. The drill instructor came up and said, "When I tell you, you will sit down and eat. You have five minutes. You must eat everything on your tray. Ready? *Seats!*"

And we all sat down haphazardly. The DI went nuts and made us get up and do it again and again until we sort of all sat down simultaneously.

As soon as we started to eat, guys started to puke. It was contagious because almost everybody started to puke. It was really, really bad. When we were either done eating or done puking, we were given mops and rags and ordered to clean the whole mess up.

We were then herded outside and shown how to assemble in a platoon formation. From that point forward, our training began in earnest.

After the first night, there were a few guys who just couldn't handle the program. Some were incapable of taking orders. Some were just not physically fit enough to tolerate the grueling regimen. Those guys were either sent to a motivational platoon or given their discharge.

One or two guys went nuts. One or two tried to desert. That was a mistake.

The rest of us, including me, just sucked it up and prayed that we'd survive and make it through to another day.

6

Getting with the Program

From that day forward we were stripped of our dignity, our rights, our ideas and ideals, our beliefs—everything. We were issued utility clothing and boots, M14 rifles, web gear, helmets, and packs.

We engaged in marching and physical training every waking hour. We learned to drill and march as one. We learned to shoot the M14 and were taught hand-to-hand combat.

The fat guys got leaner and the skinny guys bulked up. We began to get into shape and were able to do physical stuff we'd never dreamed of. We could do 50 pull-ups. We could run five miles. We learned to march like Marines. We learned to take orders and not question them. It sounds strange, but if we were ordered to jump off the top of a Quonset hut, we would have done it, knowing that whatever was at the bottom wouldn't hurt us. We learned to have faith in ourselves and in each other.

We learned teamwork and what it meant to be a team.

We developed respect for our fellow recruits.

We learned self-respect.

We learned discipline. That was the most important thing.

There are a thousand stories in those first three months. The main story is that the ones who got through all the grueling training and made it to graduation day became United States Marines.

It is a very select group, and I was proud to call myself a member.

But I almost didn't graduate boot camp with my platoon…

Because I broke my fucking ankle.

Oh shit!

We were about 10 weeks into boot camp with about three and a half weeks to go. We were becoming a pretty good platoon and had learned lots of stuff. We were lean and mean and getting meaner by the day. Long runs with packs and PT were still strenuous but not all that bad anymore. We could march and shoot and we could function on the drill field amazingly well.

But the obstacle course was always a real motherfucker. There were telephone poles to climb, ramps to go up and down, ditches to jump, barbed wire

6. Getting with the Program

to crawl under or jump over, rope swings, hand-over-hand bars, pull-up bars, and so on. There were several ways to tackle the obstacle course, the most common a timed exercise.

The obstacle course was run in full combat gear and pack complete with rifle and helmet—in other words, everything we had.

The platoon would be divided up into four squads and pitted against each other. One squad would run while the others observed. The total course took about 15 minutes to run, and by the end, we were totally exhausted.

I was nearing the end of my run through the course and misjudged the jump over the water, ended up short, and twisted my ankle. The drill instructor started screaming at me for fucking it up and made me go around again. I knew I had done something bad to my ankle but the drill instructor said he

Tim and his best friend, Rusty, at ITR (infantry training regiment), Camp Pendleton, California, 1967.

was going to kick my ass until I got across, so I ramped up and hobbled toward the water again and missed again, only worse this time—I couldn't build any speed because I was limping so badly. Once again, the drill instructor made me do it again, and this time, I didn't even make it to the water: *snap!* I just sat down to take the weight off my ankle.

The drill instructor came over and started screaming and kicking me in the side. I told him that I must have broken my ankle or something. He told me to get up and hop over the water—which I did. Then he told me to hop over to the ambulance that was always on standby at the obstacle course because somebody was always getting hurt.

I got to the ambulance and the Navy corpsman looked at my ankle. It was so fucking swollen he couldn't get my boot off. He cut the bootlaces and my ankle exploded out of my boot. With the boot off, my ankle doubled in size. The corpsman said he thought my ankle was either badly sprained or even broken.

Navy guys are fucking *geniuses.*

The ambulance stayed at the obstacle course until all the platoons had run the course—two more hours. By this time, my ankle felt like a truck had run over it and I was mildly shocky.

Not good.

My drill instructor came over, called me a fucking pussy, slapped me on the side of the head, and marched the platoon back to our area. The ambulance went over to the naval hospital and I limped into the X-ray department. The X-rays showed a hairline crack. The corpsman told me it was broken and I ended up with a cast from my foot to just below my knee. Then he handed me a pair of crutches.

Fucking great!

I told the corpsman that if he wrote anything up that said my ankle was broken, I wouldn't graduate with my platoon. I would probably be held in boot camp for an extra month. I pleaded with him to write me up a diagnosis of a bad sprain that needed a temporary cast (one week) and I might be able to bullshit my drill instructor into letting me finish boot camp with my platoon.

The hospital corpsman was a good guy and knew what I was talking about. He said he would write the cast up for one week, and when I came back to have it checked, he would write it up for another week. He cautioned me that I was taking a risk because the ankle was broken, but that if I could stay off it after the cast was off, I might be okay.

Go Navy!

By this time, it was about 3 a.m. A Navy bus took me back to the Marine Corps Recruit Depot. I got to my hut and grabbed about an hour of sleep.

The drill instructor came in the next morning with his usual wake-up

6. Getting with the Program 33

call, screaming and yelling and banging stuff while grabbing guys and throwing them on the floor. I got up with my group and hobbled to the shower. After the shower, I hobbled back to my hut and got dressed.

When it came time to fall out for morning formation, I did so.

On crutches.

The drill instructor came up to me, nose to nose, and screamed, "What in the fuck do you think you are doing? You've got a fucking broken leg and you're on crutches! Get the fuck outta my fucking platoon!"

I replied, "Sir, the private's ankle is only sprained and the cast is only on for one week. Sir, I want to finish with my platoon. Sir, I'll do anything the drill instructor says. Sir, it's only one week and I'll be okay again. Sir, the private has the corpsman's recommendations and diagnosis and he said to give them to my drill instructor." And I handed the bogus paperwork to the drill instructor.

He grumbled but said okay. He ordered me to go to the back of the platoon, try not to fall down, and stay the hell out of the way.

So for one week I marched (on crutches), drilled (crutches at port arms), did the manual of arms (with crutches used like a rifle), engaged in hand-to-hand combat (sometimes using the crutches like a bat or spear). I did everything the platoon did but just a little slower.

One week later I returned to the hospital, found the corpsman, and he wrote me a chit for one more week in the cast. When I got back to MCRD (Marine Corps Recruit Depot) and showed this to my drill instructor, he went mildly crazy but said I might as well stay with the platoon and graduate.

Big sigh of relief.

On the day I was supposed to return to the hospital to get the cast off, I knew that the X-ray would show that the ankle hadn't fully healed. So I got to the hospital and told the corpsman my dilemma. He X-rayed the ankle and said that if I could keep the cast on for four or five more days and then heavily bandage the ankle, I might have a chance. He gave me about 100 feet of Ace bandages and wished me luck.

I got back to MCRD again, and with only seven days left until graduation, the drill instructor said it was okay to finish my training with my platoon.

Phew!

Three days before graduation, Rusty and I snuck to the showers at about three in the morning, got the cast wet, and cut it off with bayonets. We cleaned up the mess, wrapped the ankle, and headed back to the hut. My ankle hurt pretty bad but it wasn't going to stop me.

For the next few days, I treated it gingerly. We'd done almost all of the physical stuff and a lot of the last couple of days was taken up with paperwork, new dress uniforms and fittings, some last-minute testing and medical stuff, shots, and so on.

Graduation day came and I managed to get through it without limping or falling on my ass. Considering we marched everywhere in our dress shoes, not boots, I was fortunate to get through it.

I just flat lucked out all around.

Everybody in my platoon helped me in one way or another get through the final few days. They picked up my slack and didn't cast me out. It was a pretty good feeling being able to depend on guys that way.

Something else the Marine Corps did for us. I went into boot camp weighing about 150 pounds and came out at 175. Rusty went in at about 210 and came out at 185. He was a fucking piece of muscle when he graduated. I was in the best shape of my life. The program worked pretty well for both of us.

Another thing that we came away with was pretty interesting. Neither Rusty nor I was afraid of anything, and there wasn't much we felt we couldn't do. You have to experience that to fully understand it.

There were also some surprising changes during this time involving my relationship with my family. During boot camp I wrote regularly to my mother, she responded with the same regularity, and our relationship grew closer. Both my mother and her idiot husband came to the boot camp graduation at MCRD San Diego and it went okay with smiles all around.

I think my mother mellowed after I left home, and I know that I certainly did. Her dork husband didn't change—he would never be my favorite person. But we at least tolerated each other after that.

After boot camp, my mother mellowed even more and our relationship continued to improve. She stayed interested, concerned, and supportive throughout my military career, and in fact we were very close from then onward and for years to come.

Maybe in the end I just needed to get away from Santa Cruz and all the emotional baggage that place held for me. There was no doubt joining the Marine Corps proved to be a hugely positive step for me.

As I think back on it now, my problems with my family prior to enlisting in the USMC were intense. My family had, quite frankly, had it with me. It was not that they didn't care about me or my feelings, but I think they were tired of the intense friction and they worried about me and where I would end up in life.

The relief they all expressed when I told them I was joining the Marine Corps was amazingly palpable to me at that moment. Sobering, to say the least, not to mention unexpected and hurtful.

But when I was in boot camp, I had some long, sleepless nights with a lot of time to think. I thought a lot about the commitment I had made to the USMC. I also thought about how I had disassociated myself from my family but was now starting to realize that they were, quite possibly, my lifeline, my connection to the outside world.

6. Getting with the Program

I could compare it to something like hating everybody on the cruise ship you are on ... until the ship starts to sink. Then everyone needs everyone else just to survive.

It's important to remember that boot camp was designed by the USMC with the sole objective of turning boys not just into men, but into warriors. It was a good plan and it worked. This total disassociation from the real world worked to perfection, and the USMC got your attention and accomplished their goal.

The "swarf" or collateral damage to the young men who could not "accept the program" or "get with the program" or who were just plain terrified was both stunning and sobering. Two guys tried to desert the second night of boot camp. One tried the main gate—that was a bust and he was sent to the brig. The second guy went over the fence and onto Lindbergh Field (San Diego), which bordered the Marine Corps Recruit Depot. I'm not sure what happened to him.

The rest of the recruits got with the program and survived boot camp. But once again, when you feel that you are cast out on the sea without a raft, any help or association with an outside entity would be welcome, offering the chance for change and survival. I think that is where my family interactions and subsequent better relationships came from. Whatever the source, I am grateful that the Marine Corps also helped me turn that part of my life around.

* * *

After boot camp, we went to infantry training regiment (ITR) at Camp Pendleton. There, we were taught to be infantrymen. In the Marine Corps, you are an infantryman first and everything else second. We learned to shoot almost every weapon in the Marine Corps arsenal. We learned how to survive in the bush. We practiced escape and evasion tactics. We mastered self-defense and advanced hand-to-hand combat. We were taken out in trucks in the middle of the night, dropped off with a compass and a knife, and told to make it back to base without getting captured. If you could avoid capture for two days, you got a promotion. No one made it past one day in the bush. As grueling as it was, it was all incredible training.

By the time ITR was finished, the kids who had joined the United States Marine Corps and gotten on the buses at the San Diego airport had disappeared. In their place were different people. To say we had all grown up would be a massive understatement.

My entire mindset was changing, evolving, maturing, and I felt better about myself than I ever had in my life.

I can honestly say that we weren't men yet, but we were certainly headed that way.

7

"I should have been on that flight"

When we enlisted, the Marine Corps asked us what field we might be interested in. Every recruit goes in with an MOS (military occupational specialty) of 0311/rifleman/basic infantryman, otherwise known as an "03" or a "grunt." That's the bottom of the chain and arguably the hardest and most dangerous job to have. These are the guys who really get in the shit. They are out in the field or jungle and have to put up with lousy conditions, rain, cold, bugs, leeches, ambushes. They are continually in harm's way. They are the backbone of the USMC and I am proud of them.

But that didn't mean I wanted to become one of them.

So, in boot camp, the Marine Corps gives you a bunch of tests to see what qualifications you have that might benefit the Corps. If you do poorly during the testing, or are just plain unlucky, you become a grunt. Being a grunt doesn't mean you are stupid or incapable of thought. The Marine Corps needs people to fight on the ground, and if you end up with the wrong straw, you could end up as a grunt. If you score on the higher end of the testing, the Marine Corps has several better levels of jobs, just like in civilian life. When Rusty and I enlisted, the Marine Corps had an "aviation guarantee" program that stated unless you were really stupid or could not pass some test, you'd be placed in some sort of aviation job.

Rusty tested in the middle of the aviation scale and was qualified as a 7051 Aircraft Rescue and Firefighting Specialist/Crash Fire Rescue. His orders sent him to Aviation Crash and

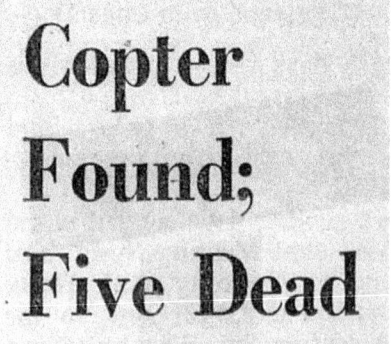

HMMT 302 crash at Pacheco Pass, Gilroy, California, February 1968 (*Santa Cruz Sentinel*, Sunday, February 18, 1968).

Rescue School at Naval Air Station Memphis. After crash school, he was assigned duty at the Naval Air Station Patuxent River, Maryland. He stayed there for about a year and then volunteered for a tour of duty in South Vietnam.

I tested pretty high and was qualified as a 6432 Aircraft Electrical/Instrument/Flight Control Systems Technician. Based on those scores, I was assigned to MADNASNATTCJAX. That stood for Marine Air Detachment, Naval Air Station, Naval Aviation Technical Training Center Jacksonville, Florida. What a mouthful!

Great. More school.

After leaving infantry training, I flew to Jacksonville and the Naval Air Station and began aviation electrician training. This time, school was a lot different from what I was used to. For example, the penalties for bad grades were more severe than in high school. If you flunked a class in high school, you took it again next semester. If you flunked out of avionics school, you were sent to an infantry regiment. At that point the Marine Corps felt it had satisfied its contract with you. You may have enlisted with an aviation guarantee, but if you flunked out, that was your problem.

I studied so fucking hard that my head hurt. If there was something I did not understand, I got extra help. The courses were extremely difficult but also extremely interesting. I made it through AE school and finished in the middle of the class.

To me, that was like being the fucking valedictorian!

Florida was great. We got to go all over on weekends and see things most people never saw. I was an 18-year-old kid from California and got to visit Ft. Lauderdale, Tampa, St. Petersburg, St. Augustine, Daytona Beach (and watch a NASCAR race at Daytona Speedway), Charleston, South Carolina, and other places. We played golf and tennis at the base facilities. We chased girls at Ft. Lauderdale and even caught a few. It was a lot of fun.

My orders after graduating from AE school sent me to Santa Ana, California, and HMMT 302 (Helicopter Marine Medium Training), a helicopter training squadron. I was back in California and my training squadron turned out to be one of the best in the Marine Corps.

What I had learned at Jacksonville I was able to apply at HMMT 302 and actually got to work on helicopters and learn more. It was an awakening, of sorts. I also got to fly occasionally as aircrew and testing flights.

I was fortunate being stationed in Santa Ana. We had a great avionics shop with good NCOs (non-commissioned officers). It was a training squadron training pilots, crews, and maintenance personnel. My teachers were first rate, I enjoyed learning for the first time in my life, and it was fun being back in Southern California, close to Newport Beach, where the girls were fabulous.

Air California operated out of the Orange County airport and flew

Lockheed Electra Turbo Props—great planes. They flew from Santa Ana to San Jose, and if you traveled in uniform, it cost $16 round trip. They had flights leaving Santa Ana at 7 p.m. and 9 p.m. on Friday and a flight leaving San Jose for Orange County at 6 a.m. on Monday. Our normal daily squadron formation began at 8 a.m., so if I did everything just right, I could fly home for the weekend and get back in time for the Marine Corps Monday morning.

Sweet deal.

The only problem was that it was totally unauthorized and totally against Marine Corps regulations to travel more than 200 miles without official authorization. But I never got caught.

Well, almost never.

This plan only ever failed one time.

But when it did, it was a biggie!

We had two pilots in HMMT 302 with girlfriends in the San Francisco Bay area. They would request a cross-country training flight and be allowed, as part of the training and flight requirements, to fly our birds to San Francisco on certain weekends. I was able to legally get on these hops when I wanted if there wasn't a scheduling or work problem in my shop.

These hops were always two-ship flights and normally left around 3 p.m. or 4 p.m. on Friday afternoon. The pilots would drop me off at the Monterey airport and I would get picked up there. They would then continue to San Francisco and spend the weekends with their girlfriends while I was home visiting my family. On Sunday, they would return from San Francisco, stop at Monterey, grab me and head back to Santa Ana. The pilots logged their hours and I got a free ride.

Good deal, right? It certainly seemed to be. Until the unthinkable happened.

On February 16, 1968, I was scheduled for one of the hops north but got tied up with an electrical problem on one of our birds. I was unable to fix the problem and the afternoon was wearing on. I went to my shop head, SSgt. Segovia, and asked if he could put someone else on the problem so I could catch the flight. He wasn't having any of it. He told me that if I could get the job done correctly, not rush it, and finish before the flight left for San Francisco, I could go. He wasn't messing around, and even though I whined and moaned, he stood firm. I was royally pissed but there was no way around it.

I finally finished the job and got it QC'd (quality control checked) by SSgt Segovia. By then the flight had already left.

It was about 7 p.m. by the time I got back to barracks. I showered, put on my uniform, and drove the two miles to the Orange County airport. You didn't need reservations in those days and the desk crew at Air Cal knew me by sight, anyway. I got a round-trip ticket to San Jose and called my mom to come pick me up.

7. "I should have been on that flight" 39

On the way from San Jose home to Santa Cruz, the radio was on and tuned to a news station. We were in the mountains on Highway 17 and the radio reception was lousy but I heard snippets of a news report of a helicopter crash near Fresno and Pacheco Pass.

It didn't mean much to me at the time.

I spent the weekend in Santa Cruz and flew back to Santa Ana Monday morning. The Air Cal flight was a little late due to fog in San Jose so I got into Santa Ana about 7:45. I sped to the base, got to the barracks, changed into my work uniform, and raced to the squadron hangar for morning assembly.

I parked in the lot next to our hangar and bolted toward my squadron formation. Even so, I was about three minutes late and the entire squadron was already in formation. I tried to figure out a way to sneak into the formation without getting busted but there was no way. I just stood at the door and watched everybody.

I was at a side entrance door to the hangar and the formation was facing me. The squadron's CO was giving a sort of eulogy and report of the crash that had occurred that weekend. I listened to this and was beginning to put together the pieces of the newscast when I heard my name spoken as one of the people killed in the crash.

Oh shit!

About that time, some of the guys from my shop saw me standing at the door and began staring and talking to each other. This started a chain reaction and the CO turned around to see what everybody was staring at.

The CO saw me and his jaw just dropped.

The formation was restless and the CO called them back to attention. I had no choice but to march out and join the formation. The CO finished his remarks, ordered me to his office, and dismissed the formation.

Guys were coming up to me, some shaking my hand and patting me on the back and some just staring at me. My shop NCO said to report to him after the CO was done with me.

I went to the CO's office and he was actually pretty cool. He asked me to explain what was going on and I asked him what had happened to the flight. We swapped stories and together figured out what must have happened.

I explained that SSgt. Segovia made me stay at the base and finish my job prior to leaving for the weekend. I came clean and told him that I'd flown home for the weekend on Air Cal and that my return flight had been delayed by fog, which was why I was late to formation. I explained that I had no idea that one of our birds had gone down but had heard a news report about a crash.

My CO said that SSgt. Segovia had gone on TDY (temporary assigned duty) to El Toro MCAS that morning and no one had spoken with him to ask if I had been on that flight. They all just assumed that I was scheduled for that flight and was aboard when it crashed.

Col. Baily told me that when the flight left, the weather north had been pretty bad. It was raining hard and there was fog and wind around the Pacheco Pass area. Both birds decided to land at Lemore NAS (Naval Air Station) and see if the weather improved rather than fly through the storm. Apparently, after a little while, Maj. Whitcomb, the pilot, decided he could make it through to San Francisco. His wingman on that flight said he wasn't comfortable flying in that weather. He decided to reassess the situation the next morning and elected to spend the night at Lemore.

Maj. Whitcomb launched IFR (instrument flight rules) toward San Francisco. At about 9:15 p.m., the helicopter hit the mountains in the Pacheco Pass area at a 90-degree angle. All aboard were killed: pilot, co-pilot, crew chief, and two aircrew trainees.

That was the helicopter I would have been on.

The CO said he was happy I wasn't dead and to clear any outside travel with my squadron NCOIC in the future. Then he dismissed me. My shop OIC said roughly the same thing. I asked my shop OIC if I could drive over to El Toro and find SSgt. Segovia and he told me to go.

I got to El Toro, found SSgt. Segovia, hugged him, and thanked him for saving my life.

I was assigned to the salvage and recovery crew that flew to Lemore and the crash site. I think the squadron CO wanted me to fully appreciate what had happened and how incredibly lucky I was to have escaped the crash.

When a helicopter or plane crashes, there is almost always something salvageable. We arrived at the crash site by helicopter. It was in a very remote area of the mountains and ringed by yellow tape. There were little flags in the dirt all over the place. These flags signified parts of the aircraft. There wasn't much that was salvageable.

Navy SPs (shore patrol) guarded the site. The bodies of the pilots and crew had been removed the day after the crash. It didn't look to me like there would have been much left to remove. This was my first experience in seeing that people could get killed doing what we did. We were big boys in a big world, and, sometimes, bad stuff happened.

I tried to visualize myself in the cabin of the helicopter as it hit and tried to think of what it would have been like.

But I could only see death.

Almost nothing was left of the helicopter besides a smashed-up piece of aluminum. The engines were crumpled, the transmission a twisted hunk. There was no fuselage. It was just one fucked-up mess. Ultimately there wasn't much to recover. The APU (auxiliary power unit) was salvageable and some of the wiring was okay. The instruments were covered with blood but some were actually still serviceable.

7. "I should have been on that flight"

We took what we could to put back into the supply system and flew back to Santa Ana. I don't know what happened to the rest of the wreckage.

I should have been on that flight.

I should have died with the others.

It took me a while to get a grip on that fact. I don't believe I've ever really gotten over it.

To this day, I think about that crash every time I fly.

You can't make this shit up.

8

Orders for WestPac

I'd been at HMMT 302 for about seven months, continuing to learn about helicopters and electronics. Of course, given that it was now 1968, I had been thinking a lot about the war in Vietnam. It was a scary place; guys were getting killed and planes shot down. Part of me said to stay where I was, where I had a pretty good chance of not being sent to Vietnam. But another part of me wanted to go see for myself what this whole war deal was all about. I wanted to experience the feeling and emotion of war. It wasn't that I didn't want the war to pass me by, but … I didn't want the war to pass me by. Like most of my group, I was young and brave and fearless and figured that I couldn't "get dead," which was how guys expressed it.

About once a month, the squadron posted duty assignment requests. The next time my squadron posted the volunteer list for WestPac, I volunteered. (WestPac stood for Western Pacific—meaning Vietnam.) It was that easy.

I've never regretted that decision.

It was August 22, 1968. I was 20 years old.

I went on leave and after that took a bus to Travis AFB, got on a Saturn Airways plane to Honolulu and then on to Okinawa. At Okinawa I got a bunch of shots, got on a Pan Am plane and flew to Danang.

When I got off the plane in Danang, the first thing that hit me was the smell—it was terrible. The whole place was hot, muggy, and humid beyond belief. Standing there, I realized I was finally, actually in Vietnam. I should have been scared to death, but instead I felt as if I were starting a new adventure.

I spent one night in Danang and then got my orders to Quang Tri. And then it was official—I was now serving as a Marine in Vietnam. Total time from signing up to arriving in country was about two and a half weeks.

I was assigned to the First Marine Air Wing, Provisional Marine Air Group 39, Marine Medium Helicopter Squadron 262. It was written like this: 1st MAW, PMAG 39, HMM 262. HMM 262 was a squadron of about 24 Boeing CH-46D Sea Knight helicopters, just like we had in Santa Ana.

8. Orders for WestPac

Troop lift from Vandegrift Combat Base, Quang Tri province, Vietnam, November 1968 (Tim Fortner Collection, Vietnam Center and Archive, Texas Tech University).

The CH-46D Sea Knight was a sturdy and reliable aircraft, an all-weather, day-or-night, dual-piloted, tandem rotor helicopter designed by Boeing. The CH-46D's primary mission was to rapidly disperse combat troops, support equipment, and supplies from amphibious ships and established airfields. Top speed was 165 mph and the range approximately 400 miles. The cabin could accommodate 25 troops and/or crewmembers or 15 litters and two crewmembers or medical attendants. The cabin could also be used for carrying cargo. All in all, the CH-46D Sea Knight was a very neat aircraft that served the USMC very well.

HMM 262 was located in Quang Tri Province, 17 miles south of the Demilitarized Zone. The REMFs (rear echelon mother fuckers) in Danang who issued me the orders to Quang Tri and HMM 262 got a big kick out of telling me how far north I was and that I was going to get shot at. They warned me that the VC (Viet Cong) were everywhere.

When I later thought about the REMFs, I felt kind of sorry for them. They sat on their fat asses in a secure environment, without ever having to worry about getting shot at, had air-conditioned barracks and good chow halls and pretended they were in a war. They held a little power in giving out orders to various locations in South Vietnam and acted like gods. Well, they weren't gods. They were office people, paper pushers, secretaries.

They never really "saw" or "did" anything war related. They never experienced shooting or saw blood or death. They certainly never pissed themselves from fear.

I'm sure when they returned home from Vietnam, they had lots of war stories about how they jumped on a grenade or killed a lot of "Cong" or shot a bunch of "Victor Charley." I hope they all got jobs with their local school districts when they got out.

Later, after I had been "in country" for a while and had flown a lot of missions, I began to realize just how fortunate I was as well. So many guys had it worse than I did. I worked in a clean, secure shop at a reasonably secure air base. Most of the time I had set hours to work. I had a warm and dry place to sleep. I had a chow hall to go to. I had a PX to visit. There was a base laundry that did our clothes about once a week. Sure, I was in Vietnam, but it could have been a lot worse.

The grunts, the infantry, had it really bad. Their living conditions were terrible. Foxholes, trenches, bunkers, tents, living under ponchos. The conditions in the field were awful. If they slept, it was in the dirt, and they were wet a lot of the time and worked 24/7. They got shot at all the time, got ambushed, got the shits, got malaria. Their clothes were never dry. They got jungle rot and trench foot. They patrolled enemy-controlled jungles. They crossed swamps and picked leeches off their bodies. The only hot food they got came when we resupplied them on certain days, which wasn't very often. They spent a lot of time in the field and a lot of them got wounded or died.

Compared to what the Marine infantrymen had to endure, I had it good. How those guys did that for 13 months is something I have never figured out. The infantry is the backbone of the United States Marine Corps and those guys were and still are my heroes.

* * *

When I first got to Vietnam and was assigned to my avionics shop, it looked like I was going to have a pretty easy tour. The guys in the shop were all pretty cool and the OIC (officer in charge) and NCOIC were there to do their time and run a good shop. I knew some of the guys from stateside and

8. Orders for WestPac

felt comfortable right away. We did lots of electronic repairs and kept the birds flying. There were normal electrical and electronic problems, along with repairing bullet holes in wiring looms, and other tasks. My shop was first rate and the entire group was good to be with.

While assigned to a maintenance shop, you were also eligible to apply for flight status as an air crewman or door gunner. There were several advantages to this plan. The first was that you got flight pay in addition to your normal pay rate, overseas pay, hazardous duty pay, and so on, and this was quite a lot of money. The second advantage was that it was so much cooler and less humid when you were flying around. There was circulating air, and at more than a thousand feet in the air, the humidity and temperature were lower. I signed up, learned how to shoot and clean a .50-caliber machine gun, and away I went.

The Browning .50-caliber machine gun ("fifty-cal" or ".50-cal") was really something. A .50-cal was big and weighed about 80 pounds. It was air cooled and capable of a 500-round-per-minute firing rate. It shot one-half-inch-diameter HE (high explosive), armor-piercing, incendiary, and standard ball rounds. It was a really destructive gun. It was mounted in each of the side windows of the CH-46 and fit into a post and gimbal for full range of fire. It was really loud, and when fired, it shook the helicopter's airframe like crazy! It ejected shells all over the place, and at the end of a strike, you were literally slipping and sliding on shell casings.

The .50-cal's accuracy was good but not great. But what it lacked in accuracy it made up for in delivery. It was possible to cut down a small tree with it, but you could also overheat and wear out the barrel by holding the trigger down if you weren't careful. You were taught to fire "bursts" of one to two seconds and then let it rest. Every fifth round was a tracer so you could tell where your rounds were going. This all made for great fun and games and the gunners in my squadron became very good at what they did. After a little practice, you could hit what you were aiming at from a pretty far distance, even when the helicopter was moving and jinking.

If you saw muzzle flashes or tracers coming at you, you became an even better shot. Muzzle flashes from the ground and tree line meant the obvious—somebody was shooting at you. This had the effect of making the gunners real accurate in returning fire. The idea was to pump .50-cal rounds at the muzzle flashes until they stopped. If you couldn't knock out the people shooting at you, you were in big trouble.

A .50-caliber round is big. The shell casing is big and so is the bullet. A half-inch bullet packing a lot of power behind it will destroy just about anything, including penetrating light armor. One hit from a .50-caliber round and there was unlikely to be any tomorrow for the recipient.

When it came time to fly, you would go to the armory and check out a .50-cal, a bullet bouncer, and a .38-caliber pistol. The bullet bouncer consisted of two really heavy pieces of steel sewn into canvas coverings. There was a front and back that had Velcro attachment straps at the shoulders and sides. It was like a breastplate, front and back. It covered from just below your throat to your hips with a small gap on each side. It was said that it could stop a bullet of less than .50-cal and that was proven a few times. It weighed a fucking ton; I think about 30 pounds. We all checked out two bouncers. We wore one and sat on the other one so that we wouldn't get shot in the ass (or balls) from below. You'd take the .50-cal, four .50-cal ammo boxes with 100 rounds each, and the bullet bouncers out to the bird and set it all up. The flight schedules were posted a day or so in advance so you knew roughly what type of mission you'd be flying when your rotation came up.

There were many different types of flights and missions including resupply, troop insertions and extractions, med-evacs, supply runs for the squadron, VIP hops, test hops, and others. Depending on the workloads in my shop and the need for flights to support the war, I was normally able to fly three or four days a week and log maybe 10 or more missions a week. It sounds like a lot of flying now, but it didn't seem so at the time. It was easy for someone flying to get more than 500 missions. I think the Marine Corps counted the missions differently than in World War II. If we flew to 10 different places in a day, it counted as 10 missions or "sorties." We did that a lot.

Most of the missions we flew bordered on boring. Resupply missions represented the top of the list in number of missions flown by far. Essentially, you would launch from Quang Tri with a load of supplies in either an external sling or inside the bird. Those supplies would go out to one of the supply bases. Or you would go to one of the outer supply bases, pick up a load and drop it at a firebase or a temporary position or troop deployment. Most of these loads were done with a sling. Sometimes we'd load supplies inside, land, and then off-load at a fire support base.

Mail and hot food were always carried internally. These missions were vital to the troops and kept them supplied with food, ammo, and everything else they needed to operate in the field. These missions were also repetitious and boring and there was rarely any enemy fire.

Some of our missions were for med-evacs. Normal med-evacs were for stuff like jungle rot, cuts or lacerations, fevers, minor wounds, and the like. These were handled as necessary and normally during resupply missions. We'd drop these guys at a local med facility or back at Quang Tri for treatment.

Emergency med-evacs could be just about anything from wounds sustained in an active firefight to a broken leg from falling off a bunker—we never knew until we got airborne. When the emergency med-evac was because of enemy fire and the unit was engaged, the pucker factor meter would peg.

8. Orders for WestPac

Other missions were for troop insertions and extractions. These were actually kind of fun. We would load up troops and fly them to a landing zone. Most of the time the LZs were prepped by bombers or arty (artillery) before we got there and were pretty quiet. We would land and off-load the troops and then lift off. But the Viet Cong and North Vietnamese Army Regulars were sneaky little bastards, very smart, and they had our tactics pretty well figured out. Even though we staggered intervals and directions of approach to an LZ, we sometimes came under small arms fire or mortar attack. These attacks were normally short in duration because we always had air cover. If we got shot at, an air strike on the enemy was normally almost instantaneous. Sometimes we took hits and sometimes we didn't.

Sometimes the CH-46s crashed or were downed by enemy fire.

Sometimes people died. Then it stopped being fun.

Scheduled troop extractions were similar to the insertions and we almost never got shot at. But if we launched on an emergency troop extraction, the game changed. An emergency extraction could be pretty scary and almost always resulted in enemy activity of some sort. When we launched on an emergency troop extraction, we pretty much knew there'd be trouble. If the zone was hot when we got there, we waited until arty or air strikes quieted down the activity, then we landed and made the extraction. These landings were of very short duration, for obvious reasons. We would land and the troops would board and we would lift off at max rate and low level away. Ten to 15 seconds was the norm.

The scariest mission was an emergency Force Recon extraction at night. Force Recon was the Marine Corps' version of the Army's Green Berets and the Navy's SEALs, but better. Force Recon guys went to jump school, were trained in SCUBA, learned in-close fighting, knew how to kill in numerous different ways, and did all sorts of other really nasty stuff. You never, ever messed with these guys.

Their units operated in small teams and went into really dangerous and scary places and carried out recon operations, among other things. Force Recon was almost constantly forward deployed. In Vietnam, they would be in the jungle for days or weeks, moving around undetected, often in very close proximity to the enemy. The term "bad ass" was invented for these people.

Nothing good ever happened in an emergency Force Recon extraction—day or night. I was only involved in two emergency extractions, but that was enough. This was always a case of these guys needing to get out of a bad place and a bad situation in a fucking hurry. It was also always a case of us going in to get them unless the zone was being overrun. When we launched on an emergency extraction, it got really tense with the aircrew.

We knew in advance what the situation was for the guys on the ground and what the enemy activity was. We knew if the zone was "hot" or "secure."

The FAC (forward air controller) pilots would be radioing in the situation, and we normally had fighter cover or attack helicopter cover. When it came time to drop into the extraction zone, we would turn off all of our interior and anti-collision lights and pull the circuit breakers on the "hard landing" light sensors.

Hard landing light sensors are basically an "inertia switch" that activates the helicopter's interior cabin lights when a hard landing occurs. This alerts the pilot that he has hit the ground really hard and alerts the maintenance crews that the helicopter has had a serious jolt to the airframe. A hard landing inspection is then carried out to check the helicopter for stress and structural damage.

Pulling the circuit breakers on a night mission was the norm. When you hit hard at night, you didn't want the helicopter lit up, making it an even easier target for the enemy than it already was. Most hard landings weren't reported—for various reasons.

At night, the guys on the ground would normally try to signal us their exact position by means of flashlights or, preferably, strobe lights. They would also try to let us know where the bad guys were. Obviously, they couldn't use smoke at night. But the gooks had flashlights, too. This made things interesting. We had different codes and phrases worked out to make sure we were landing among the right group. This is where the pilots really earned their money.

When we landed in the zone, the rear ramp would already be down and the five or six guys in the Force Recon team would run in and take positions at the side windows. If the zone became hot, everybody would start firing out the windows—M16s, M60s, .50-cals, and whatever else we had that would fire. It was fucking incredible how much firepower would come out of the bird. Normally the guys we picked up were all camo painted, sweaty, smelly, cut up, and pretty scared. We would exit the zone and low level away. Once the guys we picked up knew we were clear and realized they weren't dead, they always erupted in cheers and hugs and backslapping and went to the front and shook the pilots' hands. They shook our hands and smiled a lot. When we landed and the engines were shut down, they would tell us why they needed to get out and how thankful they were. Some of their stories were absolutely chilling. Our aircrews felt fantastic when we were able to pull guys out like that. It made the job worthwhile for all of us.

But there were times we couldn't get a Force Recon team out.

And then it didn't feel so good.

Sometimes, too, the recon teams had casualties that they hadn't been able to take care of due to being chased around the jungle by the VC or NVA. Sometimes we'd launch with a corpsman on board just in case that happened. The medical guys determined if we needed to get the wounded to a hospital ship or a nearby ground medical unit. When we didn't have any medical help on board, the crew did what they could. We all knew a little first aid and could recognize a bullet wound. We were normally able to stop the exterior bleeding and patch up minor stuff, but in most instances, we opted for the closest medical facility.

We had a couple of options when we picked up wounded Marines. We could go to an emergency medical unit, a Charlie Med (or "C Med," a medical battalion unit), back to the Quang Tri medical unit, or if the wounded were really bad, to one of the two hospital ships cruising off the coast, the USS *Sanctuary* or the USS *Repose*, unless radioed by the ground to set down and get the wounded stabilized. This was scary shit—if you made the wrong call, someone might die. Someone who might have lived, if a different decision had been made. We were still just kids, forced to make these life-or-death decisions. And live with the consequences for the rest of our lives.

9

Danger Where You Least Expect It

In late October 1968 I was assigned to resupply missions that were certain to involve a large geographic area, numerous flights, many different delivery bases and LZs, and significant flight time. One day our flight crew consisted of the pilot, Capt. Baylor, a new co-pilot named Lt. Willing, Cpl. Rollins as the portside gunner and me as the starboard gunner. The crew chief was Cpl. Shurley. First name—Marlon. With a name like that, you'd figure this guy would be pretty tough. In fact, the opposite was true.

Shurley seemed average in all respects and was slightly reclusive. He did not have many friends in the squadron (but no enemies I knew of) and mostly kept to himself. He had darting eyes and never really made eye contact when you spoke to him. He never seemed at ease. His uniforms were always a little frayed and dirty and his living area was a mess.

I didn't think much of Shurley's abilities as a crew chief. He was crew chief for ET 8 in HMM 262. ET 8 stands for "Echo Tango 8." "Echo Tango" was HMM 262's call sign. Simply put, ET 8 was his bird and he was responsible for all mechanical operation, airworthiness, cleanliness, airframe condition, and so on.

That bird had a history of mechanical issues and a yellow sheet record that was not the best. ET 8 never looked clean or well cared for. It was mostly little things, like C-ration cans scattered around the fuselage, oil spots on the floor, fasteners that did not work correctly for the hatches and access panels, and access panels that did not fit correctly. ET 8 looked slightly neglected, but never enough to jeopardize flying it. Imagine a family car with fast-food wrappers on the floor, dirty windows, a small dent in the front bumper, and a door handle that worked intermittently. Nothing horrible, but not exactly right, either.

Prior to our flight that morning, Cpl. Rollins and I checked out our .50-cals, side arms, bullet bouncers and ammo, and we began to set up in ET 8. While I was installing my .50-cal to the starboard mount, the mount pivot broke and the .50-cal's barrel hit the deck of the helicopter. I was able to hold

9. Danger Where You Least Expect It 51

CH-46 external resupply load, November 1968 (Tim Fortner Collection, Vietnam Center and Archive, Texas Tech University).

on to the handle end, but the weight of the gun when the mount broke was too heavy for me to hang on to and the barrel hit the hatch opening and the floor. Hard. *Shit!*

Shurley came over, looked at the mount pivot, and said he'd replace it.

The mount replacement took about 10 minutes, and while he was replacing it, I asked him why it broke. He just shrugged. I had never seen a gun mount break before. The broken mount had what appeared to be a crack with rust in it, meaning it had been that way for a while. Had that mount broken during a flight, the .50-cal would have gone out the window!

I took the .50-cal back to the armory and exchanged it for another one. With the mount repaired and the new gun mounted, the pilot and co-pilot came aboard after their pre-flight checks and told Shurley that the inside left rear tire looked flat and needed to be checked. Shurley went out, checked the tire, and told the pilot he would put air in it.

Put air in the tire?

At that point, I asked Shurley if he thought it might be a good idea to see why the tire was low instead of just putting air in it. Shurley got a really nasty look in his eye and told me he was the crew chief, this was his bird, and to mind my own business. My response was pretty simple: "The gun mount broke because it was cracked—your job is to look at this stuff. Maybe the tire is flat because it has a hole in it! Did you consider that? Check it out and see what the problem is. That's your job! The pilot should not have found the low tire. You're the crew chief! Go do it right!"

After further inspection by Cpl. Rollins, Shurley, and me, we determined that the tire was delaminating and losing air. I asked Shurley how long this had been going on and he said, "About two weeks." I could not believe it. I told him he needed to replace the tire and that air was not the problem. I then asked him, "If you knew about this two weeks ago, why didn't you just replace the tire?" His answer pretty much summed up Shurley: "I was going to get around to it." I stood there in utter disbelief.

Shurley and two mechanics from the maintenance shop changed the wheel/tire assembly, checked the air pressure, and checked the other tires. We were finally ready to start our assigned flight ops, albeit now two hours behind schedule.

Upon motor start-up, the EGT (exhaust gas temperature) on the starboard motor became erratic and went from mid-range high to mid-range low. In itself, this was not a terminal problem but one that was irregular and needed to be monitored.

The pilot said to Shurley over the intercom, "Corporal Shurley, the last time I flew this bird, I wrote up a yellow sheet for the erratic EGT on the starboard motor—it's still erratic and seems a little worse than the last time. Why wasn't this fixed?"

Shurley's reply was "I don't know, but I will check it out when we land." He didn't know? Was this guy for real? This flight was starting to suck and we weren't even in the air yet! Nevertheless, we took off from Quang Tri for Camp Carroll and our first external resupply load.

9. Danger Where You Least Expect It

External resupply loads could include just about anything: ammunition, guns, hand grenades, food, water, mail, sandbags, and so on. Sometimes there would be light artillery, electrical generators, bunker matting, and the like.

External resupply loads were about the easiest loads to carry. The CH-46D had a square hole in the floor and a top access panel. Lift off the access panel and there was a large, remotely activated hook assembly. The hook could be released by the pilot, co-pilot, or crew chief. The release control was called a pickle switch. To pick up an external load, the pilot would hover above a pallet of supplies and a ground crewman would hook a steel cable and "eye" attached to the pallet to the cargo hook on the helicopter. The helicopter would then slowly lift up until the pallet cleared the ground and then head to the drop point.

Once at the drop point, the pilot would come to a hover and lightly place the load on the ground, hit the pickle switch to disconnect the cargo hook, release the load, and fly off. The final load-bearing platform was usually a square net or a pallet (sometimes steel and sometimes wood). The supplies were placed in the center of the net, the corners gathered into a cable and eye, the eye hooked to the helicopter floor hook and away it went. A pallet had four attachment points, at the corners, with four cables running to an eye and cable. Same procedure ... the eye was hooked to the helicopter floor hook and away it went.

With an irregular-shaped load (a light gun on wheels, a generator, a water tank, for instance) each shape had attachment points for external transport. The final attachment was always the same with the hook in the floor. A pretty simple system. Not much could go wrong. And normally, not much did.

Our first load that day was a pallet of supplies. We picked it up, flew to an LZ, dropped the load, and returned for another load. The second load was an external net load filled with C-rats and some supplies in cardboard boxes. Capt. Baylor came to a hover over the load and Shurley, as was the norm, talked him down to the load. The ground crewman hooked up the load and Shurley said to Capt. Baylor, "We have a load. Clear to go." Baylor began to lift off.

I had been watching the guy on the ground do the hook up when Shurley told the pilot that it was clear to go. It wasn't!

The ground crewman, while climbing down the net after the hook up, caught his foot in the net when Capt. Baylor began to pull up, lost his grip, and fell into the load. As the load was lifted, all that guy could do was hang on for dear life! He was now part of the load and we were climbing and turning pretty fast.

I looked at Shurley and he was staring out the window at the horizon and not looking at the load! Over the intercom I told Capt. Baylor, "Sir, there is a man caught in the cargo net. Slow down and ease the bird back to base."

Without hesitation, Baylor gently took the bird around and headed back to the pick-up point.

Shurley then looked down and talked the pilot back down and the crewman was able to drop safely to the ground. Lucky guy! We lifted off, delivered the load to the scheduled LZ, and returned to Camp Carroll for another load.

During that portion of the flight, Capt. Baylor said, "Shurley, what the hell was that all about? Why did we lift off with a guy on the load?"

Shurley replied, "I couldn't see him after we lifted off. I don't know why he stayed on the net. He waved at me that the hook was on and I told you to go."

Baylor said, "Okay, crew, let's look sharp back there and keep an eye on things. We can't have problems like this." Okay, *crew*? How about "Okay, Shurley"? What a joke!

The third load was a pallet and, about halfway to the receiving LZ, one of the pallet cables came loose, the pallet tipped, and most of the supplies fell off and landed in the jungle. The helicopter lurched pretty good and experienced an immediate altitude gain due to the loss of the weight from that load. We returned to Camp Carroll, dropped off what was left of the load, picked up another load, a very large pallet, and headed to the next LZ with the supplies.

About five minutes into that load, the hook in the floor released and the loaded pallet dropped into the jungle. I actually saw the load fall away, hit the jungle canopy, and disappear. This time the helicopter took a violent climb due to the loss of weight and the pilot struggled to get the bird back under control.

I looked at Shurley and noticed that he had the pickle switch in his left hand. That was not uncommon because, in the event of an emergency, you would quickly pickle any external load. In his right hand was the push-to-talk button on a walk-around cable. Shurley had been talking to the pilot at the time the load pickled. Let's do the math ... a pickle switch in his left hand and a push-to-talk switch in his right.... *Hmmm.* Shurley was staring at the pickle switch control button with a very strange look on his face.

The pilot was naturally pretty pissed and said, "What the fuck just happened to the load? What's going on back there?!" Shurley replied that there had been a hook malfunction. *Right.* Not a chance. Shurley never admitted it, but I believe he accidentally hit the pickle switch, thinking it was the push-to-talk button, and accidentally dumped the load into the jungle.

We returned to Camp Carroll and shut down to inspect the hook. There was nothing wrong with the hook, and the pickle mechanism locked and unlocked as designed. The pilot and co-pilot just stared at Shurley. As long as we were on the ground, we decided to grab a quick meal of C-rations before continuing our missions.

Looking around the cabin for the C-rations normally carried on board,

9. Danger Where You Least Expect It

we found nothing. It was the crew chief's job to make sure there were always at least two boxes of C-rats on the bird at all times. That makes a lot of sense. Two boxes of C-rats held about 24 meals total. I asked Shurley where he had the C-rats hidden and he shrugged and said, "I guess I forgot to put them on board." I asked Shurley if he was feeling okay and if he forgot anything else! He simply shrugged again.

Luckily the grunts at Camp Carroll gave us some C-rats and we started up the helicopter and hooked up another load. That mission went pretty well, until we were returning to Camp Carroll and both low fuel lights on the master caution panel blinked on.

Great!

The pilot asked Shurley if the bird had been fueled and Shurley assured him that it had been refueled following the last mission the previous day. Both fuel gauges read mid-range so there was not a great deal of panic.

We landed at Camp Carroll and taxied to the fueling area, where Shurley filled up the bird. In his defense, the fuel level was just above half-full so the gauges were correct and the warning lights were wrong.

Before our next external mission, the pilot said to Shurley over the intercom, "Corporal Shurley, the last time I flew this bird, I wrote up a yellow sheet for the low fuel warning lights coming on. Why wasn't this fixed?"

Shurley replied, "I don't know, but I will check it out when we land." Once again, none of this was any good and, moreover, seemed to be getting worse!!

During the final mission of the day, we dropped a load at the Rockpile. The Rockpile was located on a tall spire of land and was literally on top of a small, narrow mountain. I think the only way up or down was by helicopter. That mission too went off without a hitch. It was now about 7 p.m. We had been at it since about five in the morning and we were beat.

On the short flight back to Quang Tri, we were cruising at about 2,000 feet. Out of the corner of my eye, I saw Shurley head for my left side at a rush. He raised his arms out in front of him and got in position to push me away from my gun.

By way of explanation, I'd been half expecting this possibility and had my guard up and my eye on Shurley for the entire day. This was not the first time this type of incident had occurred with him. Other gunners who flew with Shurley had told me that he had surprised them on missions, pushed them away from their guns and began firing into the jungle, the trees, or whatever else, and then radioed the pilot that the aircraft was taking fire. In every instance, from what I had heard, there was never any enemy fire.

Perhaps Shurley wanted to get more strike flights or air medals or just attention. He was either trying to get noticed, have a good story to tell, or simply going nuts.

Before Shurley reached me and my gun, I got up off my ammo box seat and swung the butt of my M16 into his helmet. Shurley went down hard and the butt of the M16 broke—which was hard to believe considering the way the rifle butt was constructed. I pulled Shurley to the front of the aircraft with the help of Cpl. Rollins and laid him against the bulkhead. I looked at Rollins and got the thumbs up from him—he had witnessed the whole episode. I shouted to Shurley that when we were on the ground, this was going to get sorted out with the CO. Shurley just glared back at me. Fuck him!

The pilot and co-pilot were not aware of what had just happened. I told Capt. Baylor there was a problem and suggested he go directly to the parking revetment and the bird could get refueled in the parking spot.

With the bird parked and the engines winding down, Shurley tried to get up but Rollins and I held him down. Then I lightly kneed him in the chest (bullet bouncer on and all) to make him realize we were serious.

As the pilots exited the cockpit, I told Capt. Baylor we had a serious problem with a very unstable person and needed a medic. I said I thought the CO needed to be informed immediately. Capt. Baylor listened and then, inexplicably, told both Rollins and me that he would inform the CO, but for now Shurley was to be left alone to finish his post-flight duties. Well, RHIP (rank has its privileges), and the captain used that in his favor. Capt. Baylor really did not fully register what had happened during the missions or what was happening now with Shurley. I knew Capt. Baylor was making a mistake, but I did not want the hassle or trouble of arguing with an officer.

There was another way to get this handled.

I asked Rollins to turn in my gun and equipment and told him that I was going to stay real close to Shurley until some sort of decision was made regarding him. I did not like this guy being loose and really felt he needed some sort of intervention, medical attention, or arrest supervision (or all three!). Clearly, something was very, very wrong.

Amazingly, even after all this, Shurley seemed pretty calm and non-agitated and went about post-flighting ET 8 and doing his normal post-flight crew chief duties without much trouble. I was confused. Something was wrong with this guy and yet he was acting pretty normal.

As part of the normal maintenance items on a CH-46D, the GE T58-10 turbo shaft engines needed periodic maintenance and cleaning. The cleaning was done with some chemical that cleaned the turbine vanes from exhaust build-up and carbon. I don't know what the timetable was for the cleaning, but it appeared that ET 8 was due for it and Shurley went to get the rolling cart with the chemical storage tank and insertion spray wand.

I didn't know much about the procedure but I did know the motors were supposed to be cool and not hot when the chemical was sprayed into the engine intakes. The two GE T58-10 turbo shaft motors on ET 8 were still very

9. Danger Where You Least Expect It

hot from the flights that day. Shurley started the APU (auxiliary power unit) and put the port motor control lever to the crank position, went out to the chemical cart, and put the spray nozzle into the port motor inlet. I yelled at Shurley that the motors were still too hot to spray and he flipped me the bird. He began spraying the port motor with the cleaning chemical. Uh oh!

Blam!!! Flash!!! Whooooosh!!!

The motor ignited in a huge blast of flames out of both the inlet and the exhaust. Some of the flames dropped onto the Marston Matting. Shurley was about to burn down ET 8.

I was standing at the rear of the aircraft and the fireball blew over my head. Better to be lucky than good, as they say!

For some bizarre reason, Shurley ran to the cockpit and shut down the APU. As soon as the APU shut down, the port motor quit cranking and the fire level went way up. This aircraft was going to be destroyed pretty quickly! So I grabbed Shurley and pulled him out of the cockpit, restarted the APU, and put the port motor back into crank to get the airflow running through the engine. Then I ran outside and jettisoned a huge fire bottle on a rolling cart into the inlet of the cranking port motor and the fire went out.

That brilliant move by Shurley to shut down the spinning motor junked one really expensive GE T58–10 turbo shaft jet turbine! I left the motor cranking, and by that time all sorts of people and fire-fighting equipment had arrived for the show!

I went looking for Shurley and found him in a fetal position, curled up against the front wheels of ET 8, shaking and crying with his arms wrapped around his head.

Fortunately, there was a Navy corpsman with the fire fighters from crash crew and he escorted Shurley to sickbay. I briefly told the corpsman that something peculiar was going on with Shurley and he did not appear to be all there.

After everything got cleaned up, the maintenance crew came out and it was decided that the port motor was destroyed (no kidding!), and that because the starboard motor had a history of erratic EGT, it needed to be overhauled and both motors would be replaced.

I had never met Cpl. Marlon Shurley before he came to HMM 262 so I have no clue what he was like prior to that. One thing for certain is that he could not have qualified as an aircraft mechanic/crew chief if he wasn't reasonably intelligent. Shurley flew at least 250 documented missions, and at least eight of those missions involved enemy fire prior to this incident. He might have seemed a little strange, but he would not have been at that job if he were not qualified. So I can only assume that something happened that caused him to behave the way he did.

But what?

I never saw Marlon Shurley again after that day and nobody in HMM 262 said much about the incident in the following days, only that he had some issues and was getting medical help. I remained pretty concerned about that flight and about Cpl. Shurley's strange behavior. The next morning, I asked to see the squadron CO about the matter.

I was admitted to his office. Maj. Carson, the executive officer, was in attendance. The CO told me to come to attention. Lt. Col. Brinks said to me in terms that left no room for misinterpretation, "Sergeant Fortner, this incident does not need to be talked about nor acted upon in any way. I cannot order you to agree to this, but I would ask that you consider stopping any further queries or doing anything to bring further attention to Corporal Shurley's actions. That decision would be for the betterment of the USMC and the betterment of the United States military."

"Yes, sir."

He continued, "What I am about to tell you doesn't go beyond this room. Do you understand?"

"Yes, sir."

"Sergeant Fortner, as far as you are concerned, this incident never happened. This is a sensitive issue and this is a sensitive time for the United States and for the military in general. Do you understand?"

"Yes, sir."

He then said, "In war, sometimes things happen that are best left alone at our level. Corporal Shurley's actions and behavior are being investigated. His actions do indicate a possible breakdown and he will be given the help he needs. This entire matter has been forwarded to the appropriate people for their investigation and disposition. Do you understand?"

"Yes, sir."

He then stated, "In addition, the motors in ET 8 were scheduled for removal and overhaul prior to the cleaning. Do you understand?"

"Yes, sir."

And finally, with a very stern look, he said, "Furthermore, you and Corporal Rollins will not discuss this matter with anyone. Once again, I can't order you to agree with what I am asking, but I hope you will. Do you understand?"

"Yes, sir."

He closed with, "Thank you. Dismissed!"

"Yes, sir."

I left his office shaking my head. *Holy shit! What was THAT all about?*

To this day, I have never mentioned anything about that mission or Cpl. Marlon Shurley to anyone. I later heard (but could never verify) that he had undergone some psychiatric treatment or something, in country, and was transferred to a squadron in Danang at the same status as aircraft mechanic/crew chief. I've never understood that.

9. Danger Where You Least Expect It

My curiosity was piqued and, after my return to the United States, I did some snooping. I discovered that Shurley did return to flight status (I believe to a CH-46D squadron in Danang), his helicopter got shot down on a troop insertion mission, and he was wounded and returned to the United States. I have no idea what happened to him after that.

Back in 1969, when a problem occurred with an enlisted man in a war zone, it seemed like it was hushed up or written off or, worse, shoved under the carpet. While it was not commonly recognized or well understood in 1969, I have since felt that Marlon Shurley may have suffered from PTSD. At that time, none of us knew anything about PTSD, what it was, what symptoms it presented, or how it might be treated. Little could I have imagined in 1969 the impact that PTSD would have on my own life in the years to come.

Shurley had flown many missions, and he had been shot at, and he witnessed a lot of dead and dying Marines, especially having flown many med-evac missions. I was sorry I had kneed him in the chest but, at the time, I did not want him to break free and kill us all. And that was a real possibility. He was literally a loose cannon, in no uncertain terms, and totally unpredictable. I hope he recovered from the wounds he received later on and got the help he probably needed. I hope he's still alive today and doing okay.

10

Elephant Grass, Alabama Moonshine and a Terrifying Journey to the Twilight Zone

It began as a typical day of resupply missions, with regular loads to regular bases.

Our crew that day included a good friend, Cpl. Mick Wallace, as crew chief, and Billy "Grits" Martin. "Grits" came from his Alabama roots and his deep Southern twang. Grits was a great aircraft mechanic and Mick was one of the best crew chiefs I ever met.

Along with being a genuine, honest, and fun guy, Grits had the added distinction that his father was a moonshine distiller in Alabama. Grits told great stories about the brewing of moonshine, how it tasted, and how you felt after drinking it.

To top that off, once in a while he somehow managed to get moonshine shipped to him in Vietnam from home, and it somehow got through without him ever getting caught. Not sure how he managed that. We could get stuff like cookies and cakes and some food products shipped to us by our stateside relatives, but everything was inspected.

We sampled the moonshine on a few occasions and

Tim test-firing an M-16 on gun practice flight (Tim Fortner Collection, Vietnam Center and Archive, Texas Tech University).

10. Elephant Grass, Alabama Moonshine

it was like drinking hot battery acid. After about five gulps, it did not taste any better (well, maybe a little better), but it had a wild kick and took effect pretty quickly. The morning after moonshine consumption made you pray that somebody would shoot you.

We launched on that day's missions and midway through the day we got a call for a med-evac near the Rockpile. It was not a hostile med-evac, but the Marine had been wounded from enemy action and needed to be flown to the hospital ship.

We headed toward the Rockpile and found the LZ. Except there was no LZ and no place to land. Just a large area of elephant grass or some other kind of tall, thick grass. We were in radio contact with the Marines on the ground but could not see them because of the tall grass. The Marines said the area was reasonably flat but the grass was about 10 feet high!

I figured this med-evac was not going to happen because we didn't have an external hoist on board and there was no way to land and no way to pull anybody up. The grunts were insistent that we get their guy out of there, and the pilot, Maj. Matheson, said he would give it a try. To accurately pinpoint their location in the deep grass, the grunts fired a flare up through the grass. Maj. Matheson saw it come through the grass and headed to that spot.

We descended into the grass and it was a really cool sight! The rotor wash made great designs on the grass, blowing it down and outward and swirling it a little. As we got lower in the grass, the grass got a lot closer to the rotor blades. The aircraft turning into a lawn mower was sure to have disastrous results. Elephant grass had stalks about one inch thick! Maj. Matheson stopped when the grass reached the middle of his cockpit window.

In the crew compartment, the grass was just above the protruding fuel cells. Maj. Matheson radioed the Marines and asked if they could get their wounded man on board. They replied that the helicopter was too high and they could not lift the wounded Marine up that high.

Hindsight being 20/20, this attempt should have been aborted and a Jolly Green should have been called for the pick-up—or at least a bird with an external hoist!

Maj. Matheson said he would lower the rear ramp all the way and see if that would be enough to get their man on board. He lowered the ramp and dropped the bird another two feet. The grunts said they could barely see the ramp and could not lift the wounded man high enough to get him on it. At that point a rope would have been nice.

Maj. Matheson was running out of both patience and altitude, so he called over the headset, "One of you back there, go out and give them a hand."

What??? No thanks!!!

Well, Mick couldn't go and Grits was shaking his head. Grits pointed at me and smiled.

Shit! I DO NOT want to do this!!!

I grabbed my M16, went to the rear ramp, and looked down. I saw three Marines in camo and bush hats holding up an unconscious, wounded Marine about two feet below the ramp. I reached down and tried to grab the wounded man's arm but could not reach him. And even if I got hold of his arm, there was no way I could pull him in by myself. Grits was holding my legs so I would not fall out when Maj. Matheson made a correction and pulled the bird up slightly.

The movement of the aircraft caused Grits to lose his grip on my legs and out of the helicopter I tumbled! Zoom!

Shit!

I fell for what seemed like forever through the grass and landed on all four Marines. I don't think the wounded Marine felt much, but I flattened the grunts and got tangled up with them. My first thought (really, my only thought) was "How the fuck am I going to get back on board my helicopter? This is not good! I should not be on the ground in the bush in South Vietnam! I am an electronic systems technician and I fix wires and radios and electrical stuff and have no training to be on the fucking ground in a fucking war zone!!! There are real bad guys out here with slanted eyes and guns, and they don't like me and I could get hurt, or dead, or worse!"

Suddenly, becoming born again didn't sound so bad!

I got to my feet and looked up. It looked like the rear ramp was about 100 feet away and I started thinking I would be spending the night in a real unfriendly place.

I saw Grits looking down at me and motioned for him to get the helicopter farther down. He went out of sight, then came back and nodded yes. Maj. Matheson began an extremely slow descent, and when the ramp was almost within reach, the four of us lifted the wounded Marine up toward the ramp.

But the ramp was still too high. I motioned to Grits that they had to come lower and away he went again. When he came back, he nodded yes and held his thumb and forefinger about one inch apart.

Maj. Matheson descended about two more feet and the rotor blades began cutting down the elephant grass, making a horrific noise. Grass and stalks were flying everywhere! How Maj. Matheson held that hover, I will never understand. Pretty masterful flying in a bad situation with very little reference.

When the ramp was as close as it was going to get, the four of us on the ground tossed the wounded Marine toward the ramp like he was a shot put. I'm glad he was unconscious.

Grits and Mick caught his arms and pulled him into the bird.

Great!!! Mission accomplished. Swell!!!

Except for the fact that I was still out there. This was not good.

10. Elephant Grass, Alabama Moonshine

I looked at the Marines and pointed up. They looked at me and looked up.

Come on, guys; help me out here! I was really beginning to worry.

They motioned to my bullet bouncer and I shrugged it off onto the ground. Two of the guys grabbed me by the waist and lifted. The third guy got underneath me and somehow got his shoulders under my feet, and with the help of the other guys, stood up and raised me close enough to the ramp for Grits and Mick to grab my arms and pull me in.

I pulled myself further onto the ramp and sat there.

Then, I entered something that I can only describe as "the Twilight Zone."

Once on the ramp, time stood still. It just stopped! I cannot explain what happened, but it was pretty weird. When I say time stopped, it did—totally. I had horrible flash images of getting dead. Lots of stuff flew through my mind and some of it was not very nice; actually, it was horrible. While time seemed to be suspended, I had a chance to reflect on things. And I did reflect, ponder, think, analyze, compute, decipher. I thought about all the shit I had stirred up and the people, and their feelings, I had hurt and the stuff I did wrong, and I wondered if I would get a chance to make myself a better person, wondered if I even had a future. Real strange.

To this day, it still seems like I was just sitting on the rear ramp of a Boeing CH-46D Sea Knight helicopter for about an hour, in the middle of a war zone, and it was totally quiet as everything stood still. The lighting was soft, not fuzzy or blurry, but just soft. There was such a feeling of total and complete calm. I will never be able to explain that moment. And it was only a moment, a moment that seemed to last forever. An out-of-body experience may be close to what I was feeling.

To break the spell, my M16 hit the rear ramp with a thud, compliments of one of the three Marines on the ground, then Mick and Grits pulled me forward and Maj. Matheson lifted off and headed for the USS *Sanctuary*.

During that flight to the hospital ship, I could not shake the thoughts I had on the ramp. To this day, I have dreams about that flight.

We reached the USS *Sanctuary*, got the wounded Marine off the bird and into the capable hands of the medical staff, and then headed for Quang Tri. After refueling and shutting down, Maj. Matheson came to me and thanked me for doing what I did and said he hoped it was okay that he asked one of us to go out and help. I told him I actually fell out of the bird and was scared shitless. He laughed. He also said it would have been at least another hour and a half before another properly equipped med-evac helicopter could have gotten to the wounded man, and that by picking him up, we gave him the best chance for survival.

I told Maj. Matheson how I was feeling and he reached over and shook my hand. He then said, "I know where you are coming from and, as a pilot, I have those thoughts every single day. Thanks for helping bring him in."

His words were exactly what I needed to hear right then. I still remember that day and always will. Just another fine day in Southeast Asia. That night, Grits' moonshine tasted sweeter than ever.

11

Lights and Landings

Spending so much time in the air, it was inevitable that sometimes things would go wrong, especially landings, which could be soft, hard, or … worse. On this particular day, Maj. Wilson told Lt. Barletts, "I have the aircraft," pushed the throttles forward, and pulled up on the collective to slow the helicopter's descent.

But it was too late to stop the rapid descent and we were in deep, deep trouble.

The flight schedule for the day had started with resupply and hot food delivery missions near Camp Carroll. Nothing out of the ordinary. We flew about 10 missions from early morning to just past sundown. On our return to Quang Tri from the day's final mission, Maj. Wilson and co-pilot Lt. Barletts were doing some in-flight training for Lt. Barletts. This consisted mostly of navigation, radio ethics, emergency procedures quizzes, and, as we got close to the base, a modified form of an autorotation landing.

If you lose a motor (or motors) in a fixed-wing plane, you are going to return to earth pretty damn quick. If you are lucky (and luck is everything when your motor quits) you can find an area to set the plane down that will accept the type of aircraft you are flying. This means you need a flat and, hopefully, long place to land what we call "dead-stick." The ideal place for the motor to quit is right near an airport when your altitude is very high. Altitude is your friend in this instance (and indeed in almost every instance in an aircraft). But the airport is *never* close by when you need it, so most pilots set the plane down in a field or on a road. If that's not possible, the plane usually impacts the ground in a very bad way.

There are a couple of old pilot sayings that will hold true forever: "A 'good' landing is any one you can walk away from. A 'great' landing is one after which they can use the plane again." "Flying isn't dangerous. Crashing is what's dangerous."

A helicopter has one huge advantage over a fixed-wing aircraft because the helicopter can *almost* always land without any damage because of a rotary-winged aircraft characteristic called autorotation. Autorotation training is intense, so that if there is a loss of the motor, it becomes almost second nature for the pilot to safely land the bird.

Anytime you fly in an airplane or helicopter, there is one thing that is *always* going to happen: One way or another, you will return to earth.

In any flying machine, the landing is a pretty important part of the flight. If you experience a normal or soft landing, everything is okay. Sometimes in commercial aviation, you experience a pretty good jolt when the wheels hit the runway and the plane shudders a little. When the plane lands really hard, the whole aircraft normally

Approaching the Rockpile for a supply drop (Tim Fortner Collection, Vietnam Center and Archive, Texas Tech University).

shudders and bounces and the overhead storage boxes flex. In most cases, these landings are still considered normal. While they may seem hard at the time, planes are designed to take a pretty good jolt without any problems.

If you have ever seen an F-18 Super Hornet land on an aircraft carrier, the definition of a hard landing is shown in actuality. And it happens every time they land on a carrier. Is that a hard landing? Doesn't seem so. It is the norm and just the way it works. The plane is designed to take that kind of hit.

In normal civilian/passenger aviation, there are very few hard landings. In the military, there are a few but still not many. In military aviation, if a pilot in any type of aircraft has what is determined to be a hard landing, there is a review of the incident and the pilot. If the hard landing was his fault, he gets in a bunch of trouble—a whole bunch!

Most aircraft have hard landing systems that activate when a landing is hard. The obvious reason is that if the hard landing indicator is actuated, the aircraft must be inspected for damage. This makes sense because if the aircraft experienced a hard landing, lots of really bad, nasty stuff could have happened during that event.

11. Lights and Landings

Aircraft are designed to take more abuse than most people imagine. If the aircraft hits the ground hard, the aircraft's airframe is stressed to the limit of the designed parameters or beyond. If the aircraft hits really hard, stuff distorts and the aircraft skin buckles in places. Normally the aircraft is taken out of service and sent to a repair facility or, in the worst-case scenario, gets scrapped.

So, on this particular day, as we were preparing to land, Maj. Wilson radioed the tower and told them what he was going to do, cut the power to idle, and Lt. Barletts began the simulated autorotation landing. This procedure had been thoroughly discussed and both pilots had performed this action many times. If something did go wrong, the motors were at idle and could quickly be brought back up to operating RPM. This was all pretty routine and nothing any of us hadn't experienced in the past.

Autorotation, in theory, is simple. The pilot dumps the collective stick and the aircraft begins losing altitude. While the aircraft is losing altitude, air is being forced up through the rotor blades, causing the rotor blades to spin faster. The options for an area to set down are normally pretty good because there is time to find and maneuver to a safe spot. With the rotor blades spinning faster and the ground nearing, the pilot pulls up on the collective, the rotor blades grab the air, and the helicopter slows its descent and then it touches down fairly normally.

While autorotation is delicate and takes practice, it is considered normal operation in the event of a motor failure. The maneuver becomes more delicate when the ground gets near, and then the objective is to balance the descent speed with the RPM of the rotors. But there is a trade-off for rotor speed versus rate of descent. If you run out of rotor RPM too soon, you lose the lift and fall faster than intended. If the descent is too fast and you are too low, pulling up on the collective will slow the descent, but, at some point, the descent rate can't be fully slowed by pulling up on the collective stick and the aircraft hits the ground.

This is somewhat like slowing a car down with the brake pedal—you pick the spot you want to stop and then modulate the brake pedal until you reach your stop point. If you push the pedal too hard, you stop too soon. If you don't push the pedal hard enough, you end up passing your braking point. Once you realize you are going to pass your braking point, it doesn't matter how hard you stand on the brake pedal, you are going to shoot past it.

So we'd started the autorotation at about 3,000 feet (normal procedure for autorotation drill is 2,000 feet), and Lt. Barletts pushed down on the collective and was losing altitude normally. Everything was going as planned. As we neared the ground, Lt. Barletts began to pull up on the collective and the aircraft slowed its descent until we were about 1,000 feet above ground level

(AGL). At that point it became clear that our descent was too rapid for the amount of RPM the rotor blades had left to slow us down.

This was actually fairly normal in training and Maj. Wilson told Lt. Barletts, "I have the aircraft," pushed the throttles forward, and pulled up on the collective to slow the descent.

It almost all worked, but we'd bled off too much altitude to recover and slammed into the ground pretty hard.

Blam!

Several things then happened…

The cabin crew got slammed into the floor. Anything that was loose got bounced around. The left side engine access panel popped open. The rotor blades slightly touched the driveline cover on the top of the aircraft.

And the cabin lights came on.

Cabin lights?

Yep. The helicopter had an automatically actuated inertia switch that engaged the cabin dome lights in the event of a crash landing. During normal flight operations, the pilots carried a list detailing the pre-flight check and went through the list until every task had been checked off. There were also a few items that were *not* on the real list but were on the list in the minds of all combat-area pilots. One of those items was "Pull cabin dome lights' circuit breaker!"

There was a good reason for that unwritten pre-flight check. At night, during a landing into an LZ, the less attention a helicopter could draw to itself, the better (we couldn't do anything about the noise of the helicopter, of course).

If the helicopter landed hard enough to actuate the hard landing system, the cabin dome lights would come on, thus giving any bad people in the jungle a large and well-lit target to shoot at. To avoid painting that tantalizing target on the helicopter, the cabin dome light circuit breaker was always pulled, bypassing the cabin dome lights. Makes pretty good sense!

In October 1969, we launched at night on a routine med-evac mission southeast of Dong Ha, near the Cua Viet River. The med-evac was for a Marine with a bad fever and not an emergency med-evac in an enemy area. The flight was normal, we landed and got the Marine on board and lifted off for C-Med at Quang Tri.

About 20 feet off the ground, the aircraft began to shudder violently and slammed back to the ground.

And the cabin dome lights came on! Shit!

The pilots shut down the helicopter and pulled the cabin dome light circuit breaker and we all got out to see what had happened. It was dark but we could see that one of the forward rotor blades was missing the bottom skin about five feet from the outermost edge. It was later determined that the rotor blade skin had delaminated. Once it delaminated and lost a piece of the blade skin, everything went out of balance and started to violently shake and shudder.

I did not realize it at the time but the pilot actually dropped the aircraft back down to the ground when he felt the vibration start. Good job on that one, but bad job on missing the cabin dome light circuit breaker!

The helicopter was no longer flyable and we were picked up by a standby med-evac aircraft from our squadron. We dropped off the sick Marine at C-Med and called it a night. Our helicopter was lifted out of the LZ the next day by a Sikorsky Sky Crane and returned to Quang Tri for repairs.

Returning to the night of the med-evac, it turned out that the pilot had not pulled the cabin dome lights circuit breaker during his pre-flight check. We literally dodged a bullet on that mission. Had the zone been hot and the VC or NVA close, we could have been in real trouble.

Similarly, in late October we launched on a two-aircraft flight for an emergency troop extraction west of Camp Carroll. The Marines in the bush were taking sporadic enemy fire and had walked into an ambush set up by the VC. They backed off and got to an area that was not hot and then called for the extraction.

Our aircraft was flying wing to the lead and we orbited the LZ while the lead helicopter approached the LZ. Shortly before landing in the LZ, the lead aircraft began to take enemy fire from the south side of the zone. Some of the enemy rounds hit the aircraft and it dropped into the LZ. Hard.

Then the cabin lights came on and the helicopter lit up like a fucking lighthouse! Then it *really* began taking enemy fire and hits! The starboard gunner and I began hosing down the area with .50-cal fire to try to quiet the VC/NVA. Our pilot, in coordination with the guys on the ground, called for the orbiting F-4s to hit the area of the incoming fire and we moved away from the zone while the Phantoms did their thing.

Absolutely devastating and spectacular at night!

Our lead helicopter, Chatterbox 10 ("Chatterbox" was an HMM 262 call sign, depending on the mission), piloted by Maj. Graeble, radioed that he had numerous warning lights on the instrument panel but the aircraft seemed okay. He had taken some hits from small arms fire (SAF) but he thought the helicopter was all right even though he dumped the bird into the ground.

He decided to load the extracted Marines and attempt to get back in the air. That worked out okay and we all headed back to QT.

What had started out bad was made worse when the cabin lights came on because the circuit breaker was not pulled. This could have been much, much worse.

The post-flight inspection by the pilots of Chatterbox 10 found numerous bullet holes in the aircraft and a badly rippled skin on the starboard side.

Essentially, the airframe had taken a serious jolt that ended its use.

Hard landing? Soft landing? Crash landing? It all depends on what remains of the aircraft after the incident. Ninety-nine percent of the time, the landings were just landings. The other 1 percent were hard landings and worse. And nothing prepares you for that!

12

Your Wingman Is Down!

Standby for flight missions was always boring. There were only so many card games you could play. You could only eat so many C-rations and smoke so many Marlboros. You could only nap for so long. Most of the standby flights entailed all of this. Many times on standby, you actually worked in your shop until something happened. When you got a call to go, it was almost a relief because at least you'd have something to do.

In mid–May 1969, we were a flight of two birds on standby for med-evac. We got a call that some Marine ground troops had walked into an ambush south of the Rockpile and needed a med-evac to get the wounded out. We launched in a two-bird flight with Maj. Lincoln in the lead and Capt. Marshall flying wing. It was a pretty nice day and not too hot or humid for a change. Visibility was excellent and there was little to no wind.

The flight to the grunts' position on the ground took about 25 minutes, and when we got near the LZ, the unit on the ground radioed that there was some enemy fire in the area and told us to orbit to the south until things got sorted out. So we sat in an orbit for about 20 minutes and the unit's CO on the ground told us to come in for the med-evac pick-up.

The terrain was hilly and there was a high canyon wall to the east of the ground unit's position. Our approach was from the west and we called for and got smoke popped and then proceeded to the LZ. We helped load the wounded aboard. Thankfully, most of the wounds were relatively minor: two gunshot and one shrapnel, but all three were stable and the corpsman on the ground had everything under control.

Maj. Lincoln radioed to QT base and Charlie Med and was told to proceed to the USS *Sanctuary* hospital ship. We lifted off and were headed toward the coast when I saw the flash of something going under our bird from right to left. I couldn't tell what it was, but it was moving fast and should not have been there. Our altitude was about 2,000 feet, so anything below us was pretty close to the ground.

We learned the whole story later, but the thing I caught a glimpse of was actually an Army UH1 Huey. The Huey was avoiding our wingman and made a hard maneuver to avoid a mid-air collision. The Huey was not part of our flight and should not have been in the area.

Our wingman had taken up a trail formation and was about a thousand feet behind our bird and a little below. Capt. Marshall saw the Huey at about the same time the Huey saw Capt. Marshall, and both aircraft jinked away from each other and avoided the mid-air collision.

Then it got even weirder.

Over my radio headset I heard, "Chatterbox med-evac, your wingman is down! Repeat, your wingman is down!" The transmission was garbled and full of static, but I heard the transmission. I looked around outside the aircraft but saw nothing. Maj. Lincoln continued to fly toward the coast.

I went up to the cockpit and tapped Maj. Marshall on the shoulder and pointed to my headset. Maj. Marshall keyed his mic and asked what I wanted. I radioed back that I had heard a transmission about our wingman being down. Maj. Marshall just looked at me and tapped his helmet. I looked at the co-pilot and repeated my comment to him and he just looked at me too.

Something was wrong with the cockpit radio connections and the pilot and copilot had intercom but not UHF or VHF receiving! They could transmit but not receive. I unplugged my helmet cord and plugged it into Maj. Marshall's helmet and he was able to hear the transmission from the ground about our wingman.

We did a hard 180 and landed at the site where Capt. Lincoln had crashed. The grunts had everybody off the bird and sitting on the ground. The pilot and co-pilot didn't seem too badly hurt but the crew chief and starboard gunner were another story. Cpl. Harding was bleeding from all over and Lance Cpl. Meelty was unconscious. The corpsman on the ground was trying to stop Harding's bleeding and the other grunts loaded Meelty onto our bird.

The port gunner, the co-pilot, and Cpt. Lincoln got on board and the corpsman and grunts loaded Harding onto our bird. The corpsman stayed with him. This was not looking real good. Maj. Marshall again headed toward the USS *Sanctuary* about as fast as he could make the CH-46 go.

Suddenly Harding lost consciousness and Meelty wasn't moving. The corpsman looked worried. We made it to the USS *Sanctuary* and got all the wounded off-loaded and into the hands of the medical people and then took off for Quang Tri.

When we landed, Capt. Lincoln told us that he saw the Huey at an almost head-on course with his bird, and both Capt. Lincoln and the Huey pilot jinked hard right and avoided the mid-air collision. Unfortunately for Capt. Lincoln, his jink put him almost straight into the steep canyon hillside. He knew he was going to hit and pulled up on the collective as hard as he could and bellied the bird into the ground. Fortunately, the bird slid on its belly for about 200 feet and lost a lot of the force that a straight-on hit would have generated. While the helicopter was destroyed in the crash, nobody died. Harding had several broken bones and internal bleeding and was sent back to the United States. He eventually recovered and we heard he was doing okay.

Meelty regained consciousness on the hospital ship and, miraculously, was not injured at all! He hit his head on the front bulkhead of the electronic compartment upon impact and got knocked out. Apparently, when he woke up, he was fine. Go figure.

The Huey pilot stuck around after the near-miss and identified himself and his flight as a one-ship flight on a mission to pick up two NVA prisoners at a forward base north of the Rockpile. He was flying low-level because it was fun. He did not know what was happening with our med-evac flight and just happened to be in the wrong place at the wrong time. It was sobering to think that such an off-hand decision had nearly led to the loss of several lives.

13

The Tiger Bar & Grille

War is hell, but we had some welcome moments of light relief during our long tours of duty. Recreational options were limited, but they existed. There was an enlisted club at Quang Tri and it was okay, considering it was in the far north of South Vietnam and therefore was the last to get any good supplies. But the club gave guys a place to go, eat crappy burgers and fries (as a change from mess hall food) and knock back a few beers. Sometimes the enlisted club offered entertainment in the form of a local band, most of which weren't very good, but it was better than nothing. The only alcohol available was really terrible beer. The enlisted club closed around 8:30 or 9:30 p.m., or, if we were really lucky, a little later.

The chow hall, which closed around 6 or 7 p.m., was actually pretty good and I don't think the food ever killed anyone. They offered a special called "Quang Tri Steak" on Saturdays and at least it was edible. Guys were smart enough not to ask what kind of meat it was.

When you were assigned flights or had night duty, C-rations (C-rats) were the norm. Sometimes there was a box lunch featuring a stale sandwich with mystery meat. Some of the C-rations were tolerable and some of them sucked. We all had our favorites and trading was the norm. After being on duty for several days straight and eating C-rations, it got old. The grunts were ingenious and invented several ways to make the C-rations more palatable. But we were just a bunch of aviation guys and didn't know their tricks, so we were stuck with what we were given.

After about six months in country, I was becoming one of the "salts," had risen to a position of some leadership in my shop, been promoted to sergeant, and started working longer hours. When on flight status and after flying all day, or after doing a night stint or working on night crew, I would go back to my hooch wanting nothing more than a warm shower and something to eat. At that hour of the night or early morning, the chow hall and the enlisted club were closed. That meant you couldn't get any food (other than C-rats) and you couldn't get a beer. The enlisted showers were shut off, along with the heaters. I began to get tired of that.

13. The Tiger Bar & Grille

The Tiger Bar & Grille, inside Tim's living quarters, Quang Tri Air Base, Vietnam, 1968–1969 (Tim Fortner Collection, Vietnam Center and Archive, Texas Tech University).

Necessity being the mother of invention, my buddies and I devised a plan.

We took our main hooch, where about 12 of us slept, moved the cots around to make some space, and built a bar. A real bar complete with lacquered top and Naugahyde elbow rest, a footrest, two refrigerators, and a TV mounted high up and playing Armed Forces Vietnam (AFVN) stuff. We even had a portable electric grill, which we ran off a stolen generator, along with the refrigerators. We also built a single open shower with a plywood floor and a water heater.

In order to stock our new "Tiger Bar & Grille," we stole some food from the chow hall and bought some stuff from the PX. Guys returning from R&R were an excellent source for food and goodies, especially alcohol. The Tiger Bar & Grille functioned moderately well, but we never had enough food or beer. We quickly ran out of supplies and had to scramble to get stuff.

Word soon got out that *everybody* was welcome anytime at the Tiger Bar & Grille. There were few rules, and we asked only that if guys were sleeping, they be left alone. Other than that, it was one continual event. It got to the point where the bar was operating about 24 hours a day and was turning a small but meaningful profit.

Now there was a place for guys to go after hours to get a beer or a drink, get something hot to eat, talk with their friends, and take a hot shower. This was a good deal.

Except for a few small issues.

The first problem was that this was a totally unauthorized place on base for enlisted men to drink hard liquor. An additional issue was food being available that did not come from the mess hall. The final problem was that several pilots in HMM 262 would come by for a drink or sandwich or steak or whatever. This was a serious no-no because of the Marine Corps policy of non-fraternization between officers and enlisted men.

Rumor filtered down to me and my hooch-mates about the higher-ups in the squadron closing us down. I couldn't let that happen.

Yet another problem was supply—it was getting harder and harder to keep the place stocked because we had gotten so popular among the guys. The Tiger Bar & Grille was so successful because it filled a void in our squadron. It gave guys a place to hang out, relax, and enjoy a meal or drink when the on-base facilities were closed. It gave HMM 262 a great camaraderie but never crossed the line in terms of maintaining respect between officers and enlisted men. Anybody from any squadron or any branch of the service was welcome. It was a delicate balancing act for all involved, but it worked.

I came up with the great idea of inviting the commanding officer of both MAG (Marine Air Group) 39 and HMM 262 to a party at the Tiger Bar & Grille. In the history of the USMC, I don't believe this had ever been done before. A dangerous plan, but necessary. I figured that if we could show the COs the benefits of what we had created, they would not want to shut us down.

So I wrote up an invitation and asked to see the CO of MAG 39. My request was granted. When I went to the MAG 39 CO's office, my knees were shaking and I was scared shitless. I knew I would leave there a private if this didn't go well. Amazingly, the CO said that he liked the idea of a place for guys to congregate and had heard good things about our efforts. He said that as long as no money changed hands, he saw no problem with the Tiger Bar & Grille. But he warned that if there were a problem, a fight or a complaint, he would shut the place down in a second.

When I got to the part about inviting him and his staff to our party, he accepted with the provision that it did not mean he publicly endorsed our enterprise. (But he later privately said that morale was a lot better with the Tiger Bar & Grille on base and it was a good diversion for the whole group.) He agreed to make a brief appearance and then leave. In short, this was a good guy who saw that what we'd put together achieved some positive results and had an uplifting effect on MAG 39 personnel.

13. The Tiger Bar & Grille

My next step was to meet with the HMM 262 CO. At first, he wasn't keen on the idea of coming to the party, but at least he listened to my pitch. But when I told him I had been to the CO of MAG 39, he went fucking ape shit! Now I was sure I was going to be demoted to a private. He ordered me to leave and said he would talk to me later.

Uh-oh.

The next day I was called to the CO's office. He'd talked with the MAG 39 CO and said that they were of the same mind and would attend the party. He voiced the same concerns the MAG-39 CO had and I promised we would follow their advice.

All right!

Party night arrived and the place was packed with officers, enlisted men, and some Navy guys. Both COs showed up together and each had a drink, said a few words, and left. Those were two great guys. Their appearance at the Tiger Bar & Grille was all we needed to keep going and not get hassled.

Oh yeah, about the money thing. We made a little bit and put most of it back into operating costs. We provided fun, friendship, relaxation, and a temporary escape for a lot of young men, some still in their teens, who were exhausted, scared, lonely, and a long way from home. You could never put a price on what the Tiger Bar & Grille meant to them.

And as far as the supply problem went, that was all about to change, thanks to the United States Air Force.

14

Thank You, Anheuser-Busch!

The Tiger Bar & Grille had been up and running for a while with some success. The food we were able to buy or steal was all right, but the beer was absolutely horrible. Try as we might, we couldn't get anything but Carling Black Label and it was just plain awful. On top of that, you would get pretty sick if you drank more than about three cans of the crap.

On a regular schedule, a bird from HMM 262 would be assigned a flight to Danang, maybe to pick up supplies or mail or the daily operations plan. Whenever I knew one of our guys was going to Danang, I would give him some money for beer or food or whatever he could find. Both pilots and aircrews willingly helped with this endeavor, furthering camaraderie and improving morale.

Ah, teamwork!

But, try as we might to get either authorized or unauthorized supplies, we were always short of food, beer, and hard liquor. Once again, it was time for drastic measures. Quang Tri was laid out in a rectangular shape with the Thach Han River on one side and the city of Quang Tri about three-quarters of a mile south. The other two sides were cleared jungle and an area for Army and Navy operations.

The Army had a pretty significant presence at times, depending on their operations. When they were operating in the Quang Tri area, they set up quarters and had jeeps, tanks, artillery, modern hootches, a good PX and chow hall, and a temporary enlisted club for their people. This is a little-known fact because the Army guys normally stayed in the bush. These facilities were not active all of the time. Their PX had good beer for sale for Army personnel only. (Our PX did not sell beer.) The small enlisted club on the Army side also served good food and pretty good beer. You could order Budweiser, Old Milwaukee, Hamm's, and so on. As far as I was concerned, that constituted good beer. The Army enlisted club also served fabulous hamburgers and fries.

The Navy had a small presence in the same area, but it was an on-and-off situation depending on operations in the area. The naval aviation supply shop

14. Thank You, Anheuser-Busch!

was quite small and only operated when necessary in support of naval aircraft needing parts to return to base. It was there but little used. I remember that it was a base for FACs and had a contingent of about 10 people manning a support/maintenance area and had a small inventory of spare parts for certain aircraft. There was a fair bit of crossover in electronic parts, so there was some interchange capability of parts between aircraft. The Navy had this area in place in case one of their aircraft had an issue that required immediate attention.

Beer stolen from U.S. Army for Tiger Bar & Grille, Quang Tri Air Base, Vietnam, 1968 (Tim Fortner Collection, Vietnam Center and Archive, Texas Tech University).

Normally we had all the avionics parts we needed to keep our birds in the air, but sometimes we needed a part in a hurry. Often, someone from my avionics shop had to go from our side of the base to the other side to get parts and avionics from the Navy when their shop was operational. There was a constant flow of parts between the two branches. I was a sergeant, had my military driver's license, and was the NCOIC (non-commissioned officer in charge) of my avionics shop. When we needed a part from the Navy, if they had it, I was normally the one to go get it.

In these instances, a lot of paperwork had to be generated. For example, if we needed a SAS amp (stability augmentation systems amplifier) for a CH-46, we would have to pull the bad one, write down the problem, fill out requisition forms, draft a letter to the NCOIC of the Navy support and maintenance shop, and on and on. Then we would take the defective part, paperwork, and whatever else we needed to the Navy's support and maintenance shop and make the swap. Also, for security reasons, you needed authorization to travel to the Army or Navy areas of the base. All the branches of the service did this to prevent any nefarious deeds from taking place. If there was an Army jeep driving around on the Navy side with no good reason for being there, that was very suspicious.

In my travels to and from the Navy side, I had to pass right by the Army's area. I found that the Army PX and enlisted club generally got their supplies each Tuesday afternoon. The supplies normally arrived via an Army CH-47 Chinook helicopter that would set down at a small pad near the field hospital.

So one of my buddies and I came up with "Plan Alpha." The plan was set up as an attack with a diversion and a dry run prior to the actual attack.

Look out, Army—here come the Marines!

First, we needed a reason to be on the other side of the base. One of my pilot friends, Lt. Timmell, also served as the squadron supply officer. He was able to type up a bullshit requisition form that looked real. So he typed up a supply form from our sister squadron HMM 161 (let them get the blame for what was about to happen) and a requisition form for a TACAN (TAC-tical Air Navigation, a navigation system used by military aircraft) unit. He created all the necessary paperwork and we boosted a TACAN out of a crashed bird behind the squadron main hangar.

Tuesday, rehearsal day, arrived. I waited until I saw an Army Chinook landing at the Army side and then I took a jeep to the Navy side. I drove right by the Army enlisted club and watched a bunch of guys off-loading supplies for their club. What I saw was a bunch of pallets of Budweiser beer. Ambrosia! Heaven! Nectar of the gods! To keep my alibi intact, I went to the Navy avionics shop and exchanged the TACAN for a new one and headed back to our side of the base.

Step one: recon successful.

I returned to our squadron and set the plan in motion. I'd scoped out their area and their operation and figured the plan was at least worth a try.

At Quang Tri, we didn't have bathrooms, restrooms, toilets, or outhouses. Instead we had "shitters." A shitter was a shed about 10 feet long by four feet wide with two or more holes cut in a seat panel, which was a flat piece of plywood. Some panels had toilet seats and some were just flat wood with holes. There were "two-holers" (intimate) "four-holers" (normal) and "six-holers" (family-sized). What you did was go inside, sit down on a hole, do your business, and leave. Under each hole of the shitter was a 55-gallon drum cut in half, creating a drum that was about two and a half feet tall and open at the top. This was where the shit went. What a brilliant and sanitary plan the military came up with!

At a prearranged time, the shit duty detail would bring a flatbed trailer to the back of a shitter, open up a hinged door, lift out the full barrels of waste and replace them with empty barrels. The trailer with the full barrels would then be taken to an area of the base downwind where diesel fuel and av gas (aviation gasoline) were poured into the barrels and they were set on fire. This got rid of the shit and the barrels were ready to be used again. The smell was indescribable! It was terrible, and black smoke poured from the barrels for several hours afterwards.

The Army had some shitters on their side too. Next to the small enlisted

14. Thank You, Anheuser-Busch!

club on the backside were two four-holers. These would be the objective of "Diversion 101."

I enlisted the aid of three of my hootch-mates and, the following Tuesday, we waited at the edge of our area in the jeep. We had five gallons of av gas and five gallons of diesel fuel in cans, and the jeep had brown helo tape covering any identifying numbers or signage. I also had dummy requisition forms for a radar altimeter, and a radar altimeter boosted from one of our downed birds, in case anybody questioned why I was someplace I wasn't supposed to be.

When we saw that the Chinook was on its way in, we took off. We got to the Army four-holers, opened the backs, dumped the fuel, shot in some pop-up flares and drove slowly around to the front of the Army enlisted club. I figured that a burning shitter would be assumed to be a re-ignition of a previously burned-out drum and wouldn't be suspected as enemy action.

The CH-47 had landed and the Army guys were unloading their club supplies when the shitters started to burn—I mean really burn. Not only did the 55-gallon drums burn, but the shitters themselves also caught fire and there was a huge *whoosh* when one of the fuckers blew up.

Pretty impressive, overall.

Of course all the Army guys went running toward the fire. Phase two of our plan was complete.

On to phase three. I pulled the jeep up to the back of the Chinook. We'd earlier decided that each man would make two trips and only two trips. Each man would take four cases of beer each trip and load it into the back of the jeep. We would cover the beer with a tarp and drive away.

Unbelievably, this whole plan went off without a hitch. There was so much chaos going on, I think we could have probably stolen the helicopter and no one would have noticed. Fire trucks were rushing in and I think some other stuff might also have caught fire.

Way cool!

We slowly drove back to our side and directly to the Tiger Bar & Grille, where we off-loaded our booty—32 cases of prime Budweiser beer. I've never had a chance to say this, but thank you, United States Army, and thank you, Anheuser-Busch!

15

Requiem for a Short-Timer

Getting paid in Vietnam was pretty interesting and there were actually several different ways to get your money. American dollars or "green backs" were not supposed to be used for any purchases in Vietnam. Instead we were paid in MPC (military payment certificates), otherwise known as "scrip." This was designed to discourage black market transactions and it worked pretty well. Every once in a while, the military would have a scrip exchange and all the current scrip would have to be turned in at a certain date and new scrip would be issued. This meant that all the old scrip that was not directly under the control of the United States was no longer of any value. So any scrip held by locals or black marketeers became worthless.

You could collect all of your money every two weeks from the pay master. To do so, you stood in line, signed your name, and an officer counted out your money and handed it to you. But there were also other options. For example, you could have your pay sent to a military savings account or sent home to your bank account, you could purchase U.S. savings bonds, or do a combination of these options. You could get some or all of your scrip in your hand if you wanted.

The Marine Corps discouraged us from taking all of our pay at once. That actually made a lot of sense. They advised us that it would be best to save our money for when we returned stateside. There wasn't a lot to spend your pay on in Vietnam. If you had a lot of cash on you, the military worried that you might lose it, spend it, get robbed, buy dope, or gamble it away.

Everybody had his own plan. Mine was pretty simple; I sent most of my money home to my private savings account via the military. The money was tax-free if earned in Vietnam, so I had it transferred from there. I took out just enough to get by, and if I needed more, I would change my plan.

I hoped to buy a car when I got back to the United States and this was a good way to save up for it. Thirteen months of pay would just about cover it. A lot of guys would go on R&R and buy stereos and electronic stuff and spend their money that way. I wasn't into that. A car would be a necessity back in the real world. A stereo wouldn't be.

15. Requiem for a Short-Timer

This might sound crazy, but the Armed Forces PX at Quang Tri had representatives from each of the Detroit car companies located on the premises. I went to the PX and talked to all of the car salesmen and fell in love with the Mach 1 Mustang. This was 1969 and I wanted a new 1970 Mustang. The rep told me there would be some minor changes but that the new model would look similar to the '69. Except for the fact that there was no showroom or cars on display, the deal worked the same as it did in the States. The rep had brochures and pictures and all the info on options and colors. We sat down and started to build my dream car: red with black stripes, 4-speed, posi rear end, no power steering or air conditioning (bad move on both counts), 8-track tape and good speakers, 351ci with Cleveland heads, G Series rear Goodyears,

Tim's "hootch" or living quarters, which included the Tiger Bar & Grille, Quang Tri Air Base, Vietnam, 1968–1969 (Tim Fortner Collection, Vietnam Center and Archive, Texas Tech University).

and a few other options. Total price, $4,200, but with the PX discount it ended up at $3,100 FOB Danang.

The whole process was pretty simple: I put down a deposit on the car in Vietnam, which made that the point of sale. There was no sales tax. I could either finance the balance or pay it off in cash prior to returning to the States. I paid it off in full before I left Vietnam. The Danang delivery port was changed to S&C Ford in San Francisco, and for some reason, that got rid of the "shipping charges" and there was no "dealer prep" cost as part of the military sale. All of the paperwork including the six-pack forms and DMV forms were filled out in Quang Tri. I did have to pay for the license and registration, but in total that came to about $30.

This was a killer deal.

When I got to SFO after my tour of duty, my mom picked me up and took me to S&C Ford in downtown San Francisco. There, waiting in a service bay, was my new car, all shiny and beautiful. The dealer came out, had me sign a piece of paper, and then handed me the keys.

What fun! Off I drove in my American dream car that no one would have guessed I had actually purchased while stationed in Vietnam.

* * *

Rusty, with whom I enlisted, had a cousin in Santa Cruz, Tom Waters. Tom was a few years older than us and had joined the USAF the year before Rusty and I enlisted. Tom went through training in Biloxi, Mississippi, applied for Air Sea Rescue duty in Jolly Green Giants (rescue helicopters), and was stationed in Danang at the same time I was in Quang Tri.

I'd never been especially close to Tom and I didn't know at the time that he was stationed in Danang. We usually only saw each other when our families got together or when he was with Rusty.

One day I watched a Sikorsky HH-3E Jolly Green Giant land and go to the hot fueling area. After fueling, the helicopter began taxiing to a ready area near the approach end of our flight line. I was working on a CH-46 and watched as the Sikorsky taxied trailing a spray of mist—something wasn't right. About all it could be was fuel, which was very, very bad news.

I grabbed a rolling fire bottle cart and hooked it to the back of a mule (an aircraft tow vehicle) and took off after the Air Force helicopter. I pulled up alongside the taxiing Jolly Green and gestured at the pilots to shut the thing down and then I drove to the starboard side. Fuel was leaking out from five little holes in the left-hand fuel cell and pooling on the ground. I pushed a few rags into the holes using my fingers and the leaks pretty much stopped. The pilots called crash crew, and fire trucks showed up and foamed everything. It looked like a fucking snowstorm when they were done.

I got back on the mule, returned to our flight line, and picked up where

I'd left off. The crew of the Jolly Green showed up later and introduced themselves. It turned out that Tom Waters was the crew chief and we did old home week for a while. It really is a small world.

Tom and I talked about Santa Cruz, Rusty, the families, and all that shit. The pilots were pretty cool guys and said, "If there's anything you ever need, just call us and we'll take care of it. We can get anything. We know you guys get the dregs of supplies up here, so let us know. Remember, anything you want. We really appreciate what you did for us." Tom echoed their sentiments and away they went.

Hmmm.

I later found out that Tom's Jolly Green had been on a routine pilot extraction without any enemy activity factoring into the rescue. They were returning from the hospital ship USS *Sanctuary* to Danang when the call went out. They were the closest helicopter in the area so they made the pick-up. They were surprised by the bullet holes and never even suspected they'd been shot at.

Now keep in mind that the United States Air Force, in the theater of operations from Thailand to South Vietnam to Okinawa to Japan, lived like kings compared to the Army and Marines. They had buildings to live in (not hootches), air conditioning (not window screens), flush toilets (not piss tubes or shitters), real food, theaters, and clean, well-stocked PXs. In other words, these guys had it made, and they could get their hands on anything they wanted.

The next time Tom landed at Quang Tri to be on ready call/standby, he brought me a bunch of New York steaks. Amazing! Real food! I hadn't seen, much less eaten, a New York steak in more than six months. Tom reminded me that if I wanted anything to just let him know. That night was a fucking feast and we invited as many people as we thought the steaks would feed. We had to limit everybody to only about five or six bites to make it go around. The steaks were a big hit.

This started me thinking. If Tom could start a supply chain to me, the Tiger Bar & Grille was going to get even better than it was. Our supply of stuff was still just okay but not great. A lot of leftovers, stolen stuff, and not very good beer. The hard alcohol was being brought in by guys returning from R&R and was therefore at a premium.

The next time Tom was in the area, he brought three or four cases of beer (Bud and Pabst Blue Ribbon)—good beer, not the shit the supply REMFs sent up from Danang. We had a few beers and I presented my idea to him. We needed supplies and if Tom could produce, we might make a little cash and have some fun at the same time. I told him I had put together a place called the Tiger Bar & Grille where guys in our squadron (or any squadron and any branch of the military, for that matter) could go for some food or a drink or a hot shower when the rest of the base was shut down. A social place, a gathering place, a fun place, a place to get away from reality for a little while—something all the guys really needed and appreciated.

I asked Tom about hard liquor and he laughed and asked what kind and how much I wanted. *Hmmm*, I was thinking, *this could work out okay*.

Tom said he could set up a pretty good supply chain and we made a list of what I thought we'd need. A successful partnership was born. Tom and the crews of the USAF Jolly Green Giants kept us supplied in just about everything we needed for the next six months. Consequently, the United States Air Force remains to this day my second favorite branch of the United States military.

* * *

We had a lot of fun at the Tiger Bar & Grille, particularly when good food and drink were plentiful. But make no mistake—we were in an active war zone and never far from death and destruction. Sometimes those threats even came from within.

Night flights were pretty normal at HMM 262. Usually they were for med-evacs, emergency med-evacs, or emergency troop extractions. When you were assigned to the flight schedule at night, you slept near or in the standby or ready area. After a night of either flying or sitting around for a flight to be called, you were released to go back to your hooch. If you needed a shower (and you always did), you were out of luck if you were an enlisted man (until the Tiger Bar & Grille was born). The enlisted area showers were heated during normal hours but the water and heaters were turned off at night (why, I could never figure out).

One night (or early morning) I was released from flight status and went back to my hooch. With no warm shower available most nights, we'd all taken to sneaking over to the officer/NCO showers. The officer/NCO showers were open 24/7 and always had hot water. The shower construction was like a partially open pole building with 4 × 4 posts and a concrete floor, and it was covered by a peaked roof. The sides were open about two feet at the bottom and went all the way to the top. From outside you could see the feet of someone showering.

So on this particular night, I got my shave kit and sneaked over to the officer/NCO showers and started enjoying the warm water. While I was in the shower, G/Sgt. Pleen came in, gave me a dirty look, and began showering. Pleen was a real fucking prick, a hard-ass, and a fucking lifer. A total fucking asshole. He didn't make any effort to be liked, nor did he inspire anybody under him to do much. He certainly wasn't a leader. I don't think anybody liked this guy. He was in charge of the Aviation Mechanics/Crew Chiefs/Maintenance section of HMM 262 and ran his outfit like a dictator. He never listened to problems and neither did he cut any of his people any slack. Like I said, this guy was a real fucking prick!

15. Requiem for a Short-Timer

There was an unwritten rule in our squadron that when a guy had less than 30 days left in country, he was cut some slack and not placed on flight status. It was sort of a superstitious thing but it was pretty widely observed across the board. Most of the time, pilots in our squadron who did fly during their last 30 days usually got easy stuff like mail runs and short test hops. Most enlisted aircrew just weren't put on any flights, period.

Cpl. Mick Wallace was a good crew chief and friend who'd flown tons of missions while in country. His bird had taken hits on numerous occasions and he had seen more than his share of action. G/Sgt Pleen had put him on flight status flying re-supplies and troop insertions even though he was a short-timer. I think at that point Mick had less than 20 days before rotation back to CONUS (continental United States). Most of the guys in the squadron bitched about this to their respective shop heads but it pretty much fell on deaf ears. The other shop heads really couldn't do anything about it.

One afternoon, Mick was on flight duty and his bird got a call for an emergency med-evac. They launched and came under heavy hostile fire and Mick's helicopter went down.

There were no survivors.

By rights, Mick should not have been on that flight.

So, back to the shower. While showering, I heard a "psssst, psssst, psssst." I had no idea what the noise was or where it came from. Then, a small rock hit me in the foot and I saw a hand from underneath the shower motioning to me with a sideways gesture. "Psssst, psssst," and a thumb jerking toward the entrance of the shower. Then, the other hand produced a fragmentation hand grenade.

Out I went, and on the way back to my hootch, I heard the grenade go off.

Bang!

Oh shit.

I hustled back to my hooch and was still shaking when I got there.

To this day, I have no idea who tossed the frag but I will be forever grateful that he warned me to get away.

G/Sgt Pleen didn't die, but from what I was told later, he was pretty fucked up and possibly lost a leg. He got med-evaced and sent home. At least he couldn't hurt anyone else. Asshole!

I guess there could be a case made that the fragging was wrong. If that case had been tried in our squadron, however, I have no doubt what the verdict would have been. It didn't bring Mick back, but at least some justice was done. Sometimes, during war, some justice is better than nothing, and may just be the best you can hope for.

16

Lieutenant Dipshit and the Exploding C-rats

Some of the most fun and truly gratifying flight missions we flew were the hot food resupply missions. We would take on hot food stored in large, Thermos-type containers and fly it into the field. We would fly it to fire bases or temporary LZs (landing zones) and hand-deliver the stuff.

Naturally, this was a big hit with the guys on the ground. The grunts normally lived on C-rats, and that stuff sucked after a while. Hot food was hard to come by.

Normally our hot food delivery was accompanied by a mail drop, so this made us really popular with the guys. On Thanksgiving, turkey and all the trimmings including pumpkin pie would be made up and put in Thermos containers. We would make 15 or 20 trips, taking hot food to the troops in the field. At Christmas, turkey and ham dinners were made up and we delivered those too. On some of those Christmas flights, Santa Claus got on our bird in his red suit and beard and went with us. When we got to the delivery point, Santa would get out and dole out gifts to the guys from his bag.

All in all, those flights made us feel that we were contributing to the effort and helping our fellow Marines. Very neat deal! It just goes to show that even in the midst of war, there are moments of grace and humanity.

While I was in Vietnam, far from home and family, I was still able to keep in touch with my best friend, Rusty, with whom I had enlisted. Rusty and I were able to connect while we were both in country by means of mail and sometimes by phone, but the phone was right out of the dark ages and most of the time pretty iffy. I'm not even sure how it worked but it must have been a radio/telephone lash-up because you had to turn a crank and tell the person who answered who or where you were trying to call. It was scratchy and had really horrible reception and you had to say "Over" when you were done speaking a sentence. The telephone was black Bakelite (or some hard plastic) and had no dial.

But it worked if you were persistent. The telephones in our squadron

16. Lieutenant Dipshit and the Exploding C-rats

were for military use and were not supposed to be used for personal calls. So Rusty and I tried not to make our calls too personal. Sometimes it was good enough just to hear a friend's voice.

The Marine Corps had a policy at the time that allowed for what was called an "in country R&R" (rest and recuperation). About midway through my tour of duty in Vietnam, Rusty called my squadron shop and said he had a few days of in-country R&R coming up and he was thinking about trying to get up to see me. We got the necessary permission from all the right people and set a date for his visit. Rusty arrived on a C130 and I met him on the flight line. We hugged and patted each other on the back and did the old home week stuff and then I set him up in our hootch for a few days.

While he was in Quang Tri, Russ hooked up with the Quang Tri Crash Crew bunch and they seemed to have a good time together. He invited the crash crew guys to the Tiger Bar & Grille and our squadron made even more friends. Then, believe it or not, Rusty's cousin, Tom Waters, showed up on a flight with the Jolly Green Giant crew and then we really had old home week. I got everybody to the Tiger Bar & Grille, with the predictable results.

On Rusty's third day in Quang Tri, I had a flight op and was able to get him cleared to fly the day's mission with our crew. Rusty had been on the

Tim (right) and Rusty at LZ Argonne, Quang Tri Province, Vietnam, late 1969 (Tim Fortner Collection, Vietnam Center and Archive, Texas Tech University).

ground all of his time in country and hadn't flown at all. This was going to be fun.

So I took him to the armory and got him outfitted with bullet bouncer, .38 pistol, flight suit, helmet and gloves, everything he needed, and we headed out to the bird for the mission. He looked like John Wayne and was walking and acting like John Wayne. Typical Rusty.

The missions that day were pretty normal with two or three re-supplies and some mail delivery. I let Rusty sit behind my .50-cal and he immediately "Walter Mitty'ed" into every air battle ever fought, complete with machine gun sounds and everything. He was jumping up and panning the .50-cal from side to side like he was shooting down Messerschmitts in World War II or in a B29 over Hamburg.

On one of the mail deliveries, we landed at an LZ and shut down. We normally just did a drop and go but this time we were taking back a high-ranking officer who had been dropped at the LZ earlier for a meeting. I guess his meeting went long or something so we had to wait. I was never very comfortable shutting down anywhere but at the Quang Tri flight line and worried that we were a desirable target for any gooks with rockets or mortars.

Meanwhile the grunts at the LZ were having C-rations and had these really cool little self-made stoves. They had C-ration cans with half-round holes cut around the sides. They'd cut the holes with a P38 can opener (nicknamed a "John Wayne"), sort of like a barbecue with air vents. The grunts would use a heat tab for the fuel source. The heat tabs came in certain boxes of C-rats and were mainly used to heat the instant coffee in the boxes. When the grunts didn't have heat tabs, they would cut off a piece of C4 (plastic explosive) about one-inch square, light it, and put it under the improvised oven/burner. C4 would burn, unless it had a detonator attached. Then it would blow up.

A lot of times we flew all day long without a stop. A day of 12 to 14 hours flying missions wasn't uncommon. Sometimes the pilots would ask the crew to brew up some hot coffee. What we did was go into a C-rat box, get out a few packets of instant coffee, and pour the contents into a canteen of water. We'd shake the canteen up, open the engine access door panels, and place the canteen inside for about five minutes. The heat from the engines would heat the contents of the canteen and the result was hot coffee. We did this a lot. Simple and effective.

So we watched the grunts at the LZ heating their food and preparing to eat. The co-pilot (I think his name was Einstein) said he also wanted some hot food. He said he thought we could upstage the grunts and use the exhaust heat from the helicopter APU (auxiliary power unit) to cook the food.

The APU was an onboard power unit that would run the hydraulics and electrics necessary to start the helicopter's engines. It was, in effect, a small jet turbine. It had an accumulator reservoir that was used to start the unit. The

16. Lieutenant Dipshit and the Exploding C-rats

exhaust outlet was about five inches in diameter and exited out the rear of the helicopter. The exhaust was hot and the APU put out quite a bit of thrust.

Both the crew chief and I told the co-pilot we thought this was a terrible idea. But the co-pilot persisted and found an old, warped 2 × 4 board. He placed a can of C-rat beans and franks and a can of scrambled eggs and ham into the APU exhaust and told the crew chief to fire up the APU.

I told the co-pilot, once again, that he probably shouldn't do this and he told me to get out of his face. I tried one more time and explained that the APU had a lot of thrust and that if the cans blew out the back, he could hurt somebody. Worse, if the cans blew up inside the exhaust, the APU would be damaged and we wouldn't be able to start up the bird.

He told me to mind my own business and leave him alone.

Yes, sir, Lt. Dumb Ass.

The co-pilot yelled at the crew chief in the cockpit to fire up the APU. The well-thought-out plan was to run the APU for about 10 seconds while the co-pilot held the cans inside with the board, and then shut it down, at which time the co-pilot would climb up to the APU exhaust and extract his cans of hot food.

The pilot was sitting on a bunker to one side of the helicopter having a cigarette and just smiled at the whole show. I pulled Rusty to the side, out of the line of fire, and then the pilot, Rusty, and I settled in to watch the next act.

The crew chief fired up the APU and the co-pilot held the 2 × 4 up to the APU exhaust to keep the C-ration cans inside, thus ensuring that they would receive the amount of heat needed to make them palatable. As the APU wound up and came to full power, the board, not surprisingly, was blown out of the co-pilot's hands. No longer contained, the C-ration cans of beans and franks and scrambled eggs and ham blew out the exhaust like they had been shot out of a fucking cannon. I mean, these things were moving fast!

The LZ we were at was also a firebase. Being a firebase, it had 155mm guns and some other big stuff. The guns were normally manned only when there was a fire mission going on. When the guns weren't being used, they were being cleaned or undergoing maintenance.

On this particular day, one of the 155s was being used as a demonstration piece for a class being held for the fire team. There were about eight or nine guys standing around the gun when the C-ration cans that were blown out of the APU exhaust hit it. The cans made a really loud clunking noise and exploded against the gun, showering the grunts and the gun with blown-up beans and franks and scrambled eggs and ham.

These guys were fucking pissed.

Rusty and I were on the ground laughing.

The pilot frowned, shook his head, and lit another cigarette.

The co-pilot, Lt. Rocket Scientist, was down on one knee holding his left shoulder. The thrust force of the APU exhaust as it came up to maximum speed against the 2 × 4 coupled with the lever action and fulcrum point between the co-pilot's hands and the APU exhaust were such that, before the co-pilot could let go of the board, it was literally yanked out of his hands and flew across the LZ. I don't know what damage he did to his shoulder, but it looked like it hurt a lot.

Fortunately, the board bounced on the ground and skidded to a stop against a bunker.

The grunts from the 155 ambled over to where the co-pilot was kneeling. They were wiping beans and franks and scrambled eggs and ham off their uniforms and faces. The NCO of the group, a gunnery sergeant who looked pretty mean, asked the co-pilot, "Were you born stupid, or did you learn that at pilot school? Get your fucking sorry college-boy ass over to my gun and clean it up completely. You ain't leavin' this goddamn base until my goddamn gun is spotless. You understand, numb-nuts?"

The co-pilot answered, "Yes, sergeant."

Beautiful.

The colonel we were supposed to pick up came out and we got ready to go. The gunnery sergeant walked over to the colonel and explained what had happened. The colonel went over to the co-pilot and said, "Gunny says you need to clean up his gun from your mess. You need to start using your head, sonny. The war's gonna have to wait a while while you finish up. When you're done, we'll leave."

Go, colonel!

Doesn't get any better than that!

Rusty and I felt sorry for the guy so we decided to pitch in and help Lt. Dipshit finish cleaning the 155, and we left about two hours after the C-ration cannon shot. On the way back to Quang Tri, the colonel asked the pilot if he could shoot one of the .50-cals, and the whole crew took turns blowing up trees and pieces of jungle. Rusty got to shoot the .50-cal and was in absolute heaven! The colonel enjoyed shooting the gun and after we landed actually asked us if we wanted him to help us clean it. He was a pretty good guy.

After we dropped the colonel at Quang Tri, we refueled and the rest of the day was normal resupply and, when we were done, the Tiger Bar & Grille, of course. I saw Russ off the next morning, grateful for the fun time we'd spent together.

We could not have known it at the time, but our paths would cross only once more in Vietnam, after which our lives would go off in very different, but equally dark, directions.

17

The Spoils of War

In late August 1969, we were scheduled for a troop insertion, launching from Vandegrift Combat Base. Troop insertions were normally pretty tame missions, although I'm sure the guys getting inserted felt differently.

Troop insertions weren't just loading some guys on a plane and dropping them off and splitting; in fact, they were well-planned, highly-organized

Operation "Lancaster II." Troops getting off in new LZ (Tim Fortner Collection, Vietnam Center and Archive, Texas Tech University).

events. Having a staging plan for a mission was critical to the mission's success. A large troop insertion plan involved a bunch of troops, a loading plan, a bunch of helicopters, an air movement plan, FACs, air cover, intelligence, a ground tactical plan, a landing plan, zone prep, enemy location and strength, fields of fire, and lots of other stuff. There was a certain symmetry and choreography to a well-planned insertion. Good planning usually made for good results. But sometimes, even with the best planning, it all went wrong—very wrong.

For this particular troop insertion, we launched from Quang Tri early in the morning and landed at Vandegrift Combat Base. The insertion was supposed to go off about 9 a.m. but got pushed back because the zone prep was delayed. We all sat around in the helicopters and the grunts sat around on the ground, waiting. There were about 10 of our helicopters, five or six Hueys, a few Cobra gunships on the ground, and almost 500 troops waiting for the order to load and go.

The base came under a rocket attack and everybody scrambled for cover. For some reason, the attack was brief, the rockets were way off the mark and never came anywhere near us. If the rockets had been on target, we would have been fucked. The VC or NVA would have wiped out a lot of our people and equipment. A flight of F4s or A4s was directed to the rocket launch site by an FAC and the jets blew the enemy away! Pretty cool.

At about 2 p.m. we got the word and began loading the troops—20 Marines in full combat gear. We lifted off in two six-ship formations and headed for an LZ between Camp Carroll and Cam Lo.

As we neared the LZ, I noticed that the entire area was flat and grassy. There were no mountains or jungle, just a huge expanse of ground. It didn't make much sense to me why we'd be dropping guys into a place like this. It didn't look like it had much strategic value and there was no cover.

The first six birds came in from the east and the next six from the north. This was so that the enemy couldn't predict our moves and bracket us in with fire. As we landed, what looked like ground was actually very tall grass and we kept sinking until we touched down on something hard. The troops exited out the rear door and we took off and returned to Vandegrift Combat Base to pick up another load. I was in the first flight of six for the second insertion and we used the same approach as the previous mission. As we were landing and the troops were exiting the rear of the aircraft, the zone began taking incoming rocket rounds. This time the enemy was deadly accurate. The rockets hit to within 100 feet of my aircraft and hit close enough to some of the other birds to do serious damage.

The VC or NVA knew we were coming.

One bird landed and shut down with smoke pouring out the rear. Another of our birds had major structural damage to the starboard side from shrapnel from the rockets but was still able to lift off and exit the area.

17. The Spoils of War

When the rockets hit, troops were still exiting the aircraft. Our crew chief said, "Sir, the zone is taking incoming. Get out." We lifted off while guys were still running out the rear ramp. Even as we became airborne, guys were still running out. Some of them must have fallen at least 50 feet.

As we exited the zone, I could see the other helicopters lifting off and guys running off the rear ramps. They didn't know what was going on and just kept getting off even though the helicopters were airborne.

What a fucking mess!

As we left the area and low-leveled away, we heard lots of radio chatter. There was a great deal of confusion. We received a radio call.

"Chatterbox Lead, this is Task Master [FAC], your wingman is down, repeat your wingman is down."

"Taskmaster, Chatterbox Lead, copy. Location?"

"Chatterbox Lead, your wingman is about 1 klick [kilometer] north of the first drop zone. Looks like the crew is out of the aircraft."

"Taskmaster, can we return and pick them up? Is there still incoming?"

"Chatterbox Lead, Taskmaster, zone is hot; repeat, zone is hot."

"Taskmaster, Chatterbox Lead will orbit north of the LZ and wait to effect pick-up."

"Copy Chatterbox Lead. F4s inbound now, stay clear."

"Chatterbox Lead, copy."

As we orbited the LZ from a safe distance and altitude, we could see our wingman's CH-46 on the ground with the aft pylon torn off. We watched a flight of two F4s rocket the suspected rocket launch area and got a call from Taskmaster to head in for the rescue.

"Chatterbox Lead, this is Taskmaster, approach from the east. Your guys on the ground will pop smoke on my command and you will call the smoke. Copy?"

"Chatterbox Lead copies and beginning approach."

"Chatterbox Lead, call the smoke now!"

"Chatterbox Lead has yellow smoke."

"Copy yellow smoke. Go get 'em, Lead."

We dropped like a fucking rock and headed toward our guys. We landed in the tall grass and all of the aircrew and a couple of grunts ran on and the crew chief yelled into his helmet mic, "We got 'em. Go. Go. Go!" We exited the area with a maximum pullout and left turn.

I gave an extra flight helmet to the pilot of the downed ship and he was able to talk to our pilot. He said that he was lifting off when the rockets started hitting the zone. One of them hit close enough to throw shrapnel into the rotor blades. He said that the aircraft started to violently shake and vibrate and he slammed it back onto the ground. While he was trying to shut it down, the aft pylon partially sheared from the fuselage and it was all over. For some reason, the bird stayed upright and everybody scrambled out. Rockets were still incoming and they just hunkered down. They were in constant radio contact and never felt like they were in any danger other than the rockets and just waited to be picked up.

We headed back to Vandy to wait for further orders. After landing at Vandy, we had some food and looked over the bird. Other than some grass stuck in the landing gear, we couldn't find any hits or damage at all. Very strange.

Amazingly, we got a call for the entire flight to perform a troop extraction to the LZ we'd been working that day. What a fucking joke. We assed-up and headed back to the LZ and made two pick-ups, returning to Vandy both times. That finally ended one very long day.

We got back to Quang Tri about 7 p.m. and by the time we were done cleaning the bird and stowing weapons and completing other tasks, it was past 9 p.m. As you can imagine, we were all beat to shit.

By rough count, we dropped about 40 guys into the LZ. There were 12 HMM 262 helicopters and some from HMM 161 on the mission. Considering HMM 262 alone, we dropped a little fewer than 500 guys into that zone and took out about as many.

This mission had been a disaster from the start. I felt lucky that we didn't have a mid-air with another bird. There were so many helicopters trying to get out of that zone when it got hot that there were numerous near-misses.

The med-evac flights to the zone were mostly for broken legs and other fall injuries from the guys continuing to exit the aircraft even while airborne. We were told later that the rocket attack accounted for about 10 wounded evacs and two downed aircraft, one each from HMM 262 and HMM 161, and that broken legs numbered about 15.

We actually did more damage to ourselves than the enemy did.

Go figure.

* * *

Another time we were doing normal resupply missions when we got a call to land and refuel at Vandegrift Combat Base. When we got there and refueled, six guys got on board. One of the guys was a Marine chaplain, one of them was a Marine lieutenant, and the other four looked like they just stepped out of a *Rambo* movie.

These four guys were in camo and had all sorts of guns and grenades with them. They had twigs and leaves sticking out of their clothing. They had face paint and knit caps. They were really scary fuckers. They had no facial expression. They wore no rank insignias or visible service designations.

The chaplain got a headset and briefed the pilots. He said that an arms and supply cache had been found about 30 miles to the west and we were going to be the first bird in to begin taking out the cache. He said that he was on board because the Marine Corps required an officer of at least the rank of captain to be in attendance whenever a supply or arms cache was removed. We were told later that this was to prevent pilfering and stealing of trinkets or other "war souvenirs" from any supply caches. He said he happened to be the highest-ranking officer who was available so he was pressed into duty. That story never made any sense to me, but he was there nonetheless. Go figure.

We launched as lead of a four-ship flight and off we went to the west. After about 20 minutes, we began to circle the jungle at about 5,000 feet. The pilot was in contact with an FAC and the ground unit who had discovered the cache. There was a flight of F-4s doing a racetrack high above, ready if something went wrong. The LZ was supposed to be quiet and the ground unit hadn't seen any enemy activity. As we descended, the guys on the ground popped a smoke.

The LZ was in very tall jungle and trees. There was a cylinder of cleared area about 100 feet in diameter and the pilot began a falling hover into the zone. As we dropped down through the jungle, it began to get dark. The further we dropped into the clearing, the darker it got. There was only room for one helicopter at a time in the cleared area. This would be a more than perfect place to get ambushed, so we were nervous and on high alert.

We landed and three of the four camo guys blasted out the back and into the jungle. The fourth camo guy stayed on board. The jungle was only about 30 feet from my side and every few seconds I thought I could see movement, like the wind blowing, and I thought it was the rotor wash from our helicopter. I kept watching and thinking that somebody was out there and I could almost make out somebody moving—but not quite. The jungle was dark and my eyes were straining to see if anything was there. I finally said fuck it and racked a round into the .50-cal and took a bead on the nearest bushes at the edge of the clearing. I felt a hand clapped on my shoulder and when I turned around, camo guy #4 looked at me, shook his head, and mouthed, "No." I nodded and pointed the .50-cal upward away from the jungle. Camo guy #4 gave me two quick pats on the shoulder and resumed his watch.

The guys on the ground started bringing in bags of stuff and boxes and burlap-wrapped packages and all sorts of things and stacking it on the floor. When they'd filled up about half of our bird, they left and camo guys #1, #2, and #3 came back dragging two people in black pajamas wearing Ho Chi Minh sandals and one guy in an NVA uniform. They had black bags on their heads and their wrists were tied behind their backs.

The camo guys looked at us and shook their heads and we stopped looking at them. I didn't know what was going on, but whatever it was, it was fucking spooky. The key word here is spooky. The two Cong or whatever they were sat on the floor with their heads down. The NVA guy sat on the floor with his head up. The camo guys had their guns pressed to these guys' heads.

As we lifted off and began an upward/climbing hover, the edges of the clearing came alive with people—maybe 20 to 25 camo people came out of the jungle where they had been standing guard over us. They were almost invisible until they came out of the jungle. I looked at camo guy #4 and pointed to the ground and then pointed at him. He nodded at me and I nodded back. Unbelievably weird. I don't know who those guys were. I didn't want to know then and I don't want to know now.

The remaining three ships continued to land and load up the cache while we lifted off and flew to a base I had never seen before. As near as I can figure, it was somewhere a little north of Hue. We landed and the camo guys, VC, and NVA got off and walked into a bunker at the base. We lifted off and headed back toward Quang Tri.

On the flight to Quang Tri, the chaplain began opening some of the cache and pulled out VC black pajamas and gave each of the crew two pairs as souvenirs. So much for looting and pilfering and war souvenirs.

We landed at Quang Tri and trucks met our bird on the flight line. The cache was off-loaded and the S-2 lieutenant (S-2 is Intelligence Section) and chaplain left. We taxied to refueling and then to our flight line. Mission completed.

After we shut down and were cleaning out the bird and taking down our .50-cals, I asked the pilots where we had gone. They didn't say anything for a second and then the pilot said we were in far western South Vietnam. I had a pretty good idea where we'd landed so I asked him, "About how far west were we?"

His answer was "Far enough that we were about five miles inside of the Laotian border."

Oh shit!

I'm pretty sure that we weren't supposed to be there!

We later learned that the cache was huge. There ended up being so much stuff that it couldn't all be taken out. What couldn't be taken out was blown up where it was. In all, at least 10 loads were taken out by HMM 262 alone. Included in the cache were hundreds of AK-47s (Russian semi-automatic carbine), SKSs, small-caliber pistols, Chicom hand grenades (Chinese Communist), Russian hand grenades, medicine and bandages, fuel, clothing (civilian, uniforms, and black pajamas), huge quantities of rice and dried fish, truck tires, mortars, rockets and launchers, massive quantities of ammunition, radios, documents and paperwork, and other things. An amazing amount of stuff.

As far as the Viet Cong black pajamas, I gave one pair to my shop OIC (officer in charge). I smuggled the other pair back to the United States in a rotor blade crate shipped to Boeing VERTOL (VERtical Take Off and Landing), and the tech rep there shipped them home to California for me. I later donated them to the National Vietnam War Museum in Mineral Wells, Texas. As long as I owned them, they served as a constant reminder of one of the strangest and scariest experiences I had in Vietnam.

18

Keeping Watch and a Painful Loss

Each squadron in MAG 39 had certain duties to perform and tasks to complete. On a monthly rotation, each squadron in MAG 39 was required to provide a certain number of people for the various details. These details were primarily trash truck, mess hall, shit detail, and guard duty.

The worst was shit detail and the scariest was guard duty.

Each month our avionics shop was required to supply two people to the air group. Because there were only 15 people in the shop, everybody's number came up at least twice on a tour. When my number came up, I was assigned to guard duty for a month. This may not seem like a big deal in theory, but in practice, it was very serious and very scary.

Around the entire perimeter of the base at Quang Tri were guard towers about 75 feet tall and guard bunkers constructed of Marston matting and sandbags. The bunkers were about six feet deep and 10 feet long with firing slits to the front and an access hole to the rear. The sandbags were stacked about six deep all around with a double false roof, with each roof level about six sandbags deep. The false roof was to minimize the effects of a direct hit from mortar fire.

The way guard duty worked was that two men were assigned to a bunker. The Marine air group area of the base had about 10 bunkers. The bunkers were manned from just before sundown to just after sunup. There was a communication line between each bunker and to the guard command post. At approximately 10-minute intervals the command post would call, "Post One report," and that bunker would normally reply in a whisper, "Post One secure," and the command post would answer, "Post One confirm secure," and the whispered reply would be "Post One secure."

This was repeated for all 10 guard bunkers in our section, so there was a constant flow of communication. If one guard post saw something or had a problem, they would call in. A pretty simple operation, all in all.

The rotation for the guys on guard duty was two hours on and two hours

18. Keeping Watch and a Painful Loss   101

View from outside Quang Tri Air Base looking toward the base. The guard tower on base is visible in the photograph. Quang Tri Province, Vietnam, 1969 (Tim Fortner Collection, Vietnam Center and Archive, Texas Tech University).

off. The guy who was off slept in the bunker. The guy who was on duty did everything possible NOT to fall asleep, and it was tough. Especially after about midnight, it was really difficult to stay awake. If you did fall asleep and were caught, it was an automatic court-martial. When your shift was over, you would wake up your partner and then go get some sleep. There was constant talk over the com line to ensure that all the guard posts were manned and all the guards were awake.

The consequences of a guard being asleep on duty were that the enemy could penetrate the perimeter and get into the base. There was an officer on guard whose only job was to go from bunker to bunker and make sure people were awake and alert. There were passwords (changed each night) and the roving officer would walk up to the rear of the bunker and say something like "Officer of the guard. What's your situation?" These guys normally snuck up and scared the shit out of us. We would answer, "What's the password?" and they would normally give the password. The normal answer was "Post One secure." The officer of the guard would then continue his rounds.

Sometimes the roving officer of the guard would pause or hesitate in giving the reply password. When I was on guard duty and there was a pause, I would stick the barrel of my M16 out the access hole and say, "I'm firing in two seconds unless you give the password." The answer was instantaneous: "Alligator! Alligator! Alligator! Don't shoot!" Most of the guys doing the roving patrols pulled that shit only once.

When I went through boot camp and infantry training, I was taught how to fight and how to shoot guns. I then went to avionics school and learned how to fix electrical and electronic problems on aircraft. The Marine Corps may have thought that was sufficient training to put me on guard duty and have me be responsible to guard a sector of a base in the middle of a war zone. I strongly disagreed. I had no experience in ground combat and I didn't feel at all competent on guard duty. I was pretty sure I could fix some broken wires on an airplane, but I was not the least bit confident that I could prevent a breach in our perimeter defenses. I was not trained to do this and did not like it at all. It seemed to me that there were Marines much better qualified to guard the perimeter of the base.

I felt very nervous and jumpy when I was on guard duty. I didn't want to fuck up and I wanted to make sure I stayed awake and watched my area of observation. We weren't supposed to smoke on guard duty because the cigarette smoke could be smelled by the enemy and the glow from the coal could be seen from an incredible distance at night. So staying awake by smoking cigarettes was out. If you got caught smoking on guard duty, it was an almost-automatic penalty of reduction in rank.

We learned a trick to guarantee that if you did happen to nod off, it would only be for a minute or two. We were able to buy incense-type punks from the Vietnamese civilians who worked on the base. "Punks" are like the things used to light firecrackers and would burn for about 10 or 12 minutes. The local incense punks smelled like the rest of the place so it wouldn't be noticed the way cigarette smoke would. The idea was to light the punk, carefully shielding the match flame. Then you'd place the punk in the crotch of your first and second fingers with about one-quarter of an inch protruding from between your fingers.

If you were awake and felt the heat start to get to the web of your fingers, you just moved the incense punk out another quarter of an inch and kept repeating the sequence. If you did nod off or fall asleep, the punk would burn you and you would instantly wake up. It worked amazingly well. I had to change fingers, webs, and then hands and by the end of my guard duty stint, my hands were covered with burns. But at least I had stayed awake.

Our area of observation was about 50 feet of grass and short brush and then the Thach Han River. We had barbed wire and razor wire placed in front of our bunkers and Claymore mines (remote-detonated mines facing the enemy approach path) placed about 15 feet in front of the bunker. At night,

18. Keeping Watch and a Painful Loss

looking out from the bunker to our area of observation, it was so dark that you couldn't see anything.

After observing for a while, your eyes played tricks on you and if you thought you saw something, you started to squint and tried to make some sense of what might be happening. You were taught not to fixate on any one thing but to keep your eyes scanning and moving. This helped, and you could sometimes see a little bit.

My problem was that it was dark about twenty feet in front of me, I could not see anything, and if anybody (the enemy) was out there, I would have had a hard time spotting him until he was sitting beside me. I felt extremely uncomfortable with this situation. I talked with the other guys on guard duty and they said they were experiencing the same problem. That was just the way it was.

If you really got spooked (and I did), you could shoot off a pop-up parachute flare. These flares were handheld, and you held the tube in one hand and hit the bottom of the tube with your palm. The flare would pop out, go up to about 500 feet, and go off. The flare would float to the ground after about three or four minutes. The flares were filled with white phosphorus and lit up the night like day. Fortunately, somebody shot off a flare about every 10 minutes and that helped immensely.

During my time on guard duty, nothing terrible ever happened. Sometimes there were enemy probes (or suspected enemy probes) on other parts of the base perimeter, but never where I was on duty. The only time we shot our guns was one night when one of the bunkers thought they saw something and started firing across the river. This started a chain reaction and every bunker on the riverside opened up and started shooting. It took the officer of the guard and a few other people to quiet everything down.

Thankfully, my time on guard duty was cut short. I was pulled off guard duty and returned to the avionics shop because we'd become short-handed. I was very happy to get off that detail. For the rest of my time at Quang Tri, I thought about the guys who were pulling guard duty at night and wondered if they were awake and watching out for the enemy. As hard as it was for me, I know that sometimes there was little or no actual guarding going on. Then again, we were never overrun by the enemy, so I guess they did their jobs well enough. Sometimes it's better to be lucky than good. And sometimes it's good to be just lucky enough.

* * *

Work at the HMM 262 avionics shop was sometimes hectic and sometimes slow. Cards and coffee helped pass the time, and some work always needed to be done on the bunkers outside of the shop. When busy, our HMM 262 helicopters needed maintenance and repairs. There were electronics classes at times and other duties that kept us busy. When not flying (which I could only do when not needed at the avionics shop), and when not at the shop, sometimes boredom did creep in.

While leaving the shop one night, after my work shift ended, I saw a structure being built. It was a big, square, almost rectangular-shaped building framed with 2 × 4s and skinned with plywood. I had no idea what it was for. But I soon found out.

Somehow, between HMM 262, HMM 161, and VMO 5, they figured out how to build a handball court about 200 feet away from the flight line and on the road from the shop and squadron headquarters area and the hootches. It took about two weeks to build.

A handball court? At Quang Tri Air Base?

I had no clue what handball was, only that I remembered as a kid that some junior high and high schools had a cement wall with a horizontal line painted on it, and you were supposed to hit the ball with your hand against the wall, and when the ball came back, hit it again.

In short, I thought it was pretty lame.

Returning from a night shift, I heard banging coming from inside the building and went in for a look. There was one door to go in or out. There was no viewing area. When I walked through the door, I walked right into a game of handball with two sweaty guys hitting the ball against the wall real fast. I sort of stopped their game.

The players were two first lieutenants from HMM 262. Robert Trigalet was one of the officers. I apologized for busting up their game and asked what they were playing and how the game worked. I was able to stand inside (trying to stay out of their way as much as I could) and watch for a little while.

The speed of the game in such a small (approximately 20 by 40 feet), enclosed space was pretty wild, especially when played with a small, hard rubber ball (about three ounces and 1⅞" diameter) that flies really fast against very hard walls!

After their game finished, the two officers asked if I want to learn how to play. Why not? It seemed like fun.

For about the next four weeks, Lt. Trigalet taught me how to play four-wall handball. My hands hurt so bad afterward, it was hard to do my avionics shop work. He got me a pair of handball gloves and they helped, but the only way to minimize the pain was to get your hands used to hitting the ball and somewhat callus them. Eventually I could play for about an hour without my hands hurting.

For several months after, Lt. Trigalet and I played at night (when not working or flying) and I eventually beat him in a game. It was great. We played doubles with some other pilots from the squadrons on base and won most of those matches.

18. Keeping Watch and a Painful Loss

Four people in that small, enclosed area was not without its associated dramas. A lot of time was spent on the floor in a heap, and there were numerous breaks for one of us to recover from being hit in the head by the ball. It really hurt. Bloody noses and split lips and a few black eyes were not uncommon. Bruising almost everywhere was the norm.

It was fun, and a great way to pass the time. And I felt that Robert Trigalet and I became friends, and the officer/enlisted issue never came into play. I also flew with Lt. Trigalet on several flights and he was a pretty good pilot. I was happy that he took me under his wing and showed me how to play handball and have some fun. In short, he was a good man and a kind person. And then one day came the terrible news:

> From HMM-262 Command Chronology—May 1969
>
> *On May 2, 1969, while on a resupply mission, Chatterbox 93-1 and 93-2 commanded by LtCol Wells and 1/Lt Trigalet carried supplies to XD847614. When in the zone, 93-2 picked up 7 passengers for transportation to Vandegrift Combat Base. While departing from the area, 93-2 experienced a mid-air collision with an Army UH-1H, fell out of control and crashed, with all aboard being killed. The crew consisted of the pilot, 1/Lt Trigalet, the copilot 1/Lt Williams, the crew chief L/Cpl. Pyle and the two gunners L/Cpl. Eakins and L/Cpl. Stoller.*

Robert Trigalet was 24 years old.
More losses.
More names that, much later on, would be placed on The Wall.
Damn it!

19

Extracting a Recon Team—When Every Second Counts

I was on standby for flight ops late in January 1969. The weather was pretty clear and, as usual, hot and sticky. At around 2 a.m., we got a call for an emergency recon team extraction. The recon team was in deep shit and under heavy enemy attack. Their location was a little south of the Rockpile and in hilly terrain with tall trees.

We launched and were transferred off to the FAC (forward air controller) and the recon unit to apprise us of the situation. The pilot for this mission was Maj. Pentor. He was a no-nonsense guy, a fabulous helicopter pilot, and could fly any type of mission—I really enjoyed flying with him. We headed toward the Rockpile and were given the location of the recon team. As we neared their location, we could see muzzle flashes and tracers on the ground coupled with a few small flashes that I figured must be hand grenades.

The FAC told us to pull off and worked with the recon team leader to call in an air strike on the Viet Cong or NVA (North Vietnamese Army). A flight of two A4s hammered the area for a few minutes and it appeared that they'd killed the bad guys. It was quite a show at night and from above.

The recon team leader told our pilot, Maj. Pentor, that he had a team of six with one seriously wounded and one with minor wounds. He radioed he thought the gooks were gone but wanted us to wait a few minutes while he sent somebody to check out the situation. He called back and said that he couldn't confirm the zone was safe but that he badly wanted to get himself and his team out of there.

Maj. Pentor began his approach with all clearance lights out. It was pitch-black. He called the recon team leader and asked for guidance. The recon team leader told us to come right a little and that he and his team were about one klick directly in front. A flashlight began signaling in front of us and Maj. Pentor radioed to the recon team leader, "Black Bart, I have a light at my one o'clock; is that you?"

19. Extracting a Recon Team—When Every Second Counts

Commanding officer of HMM 262 awarding Tim the Air Medal for "Meritorious achievement in flights as an aerial gunner during emergency med evac mission under hostile conditions," November 13, 1968 (Tim Fortner Collection, Vietnam Center and Archive, Texas Tech University).

"Negative Chatterbox Six, *We are not signaling! It isn't us! Repeat—it isn't us!*"

Maj. Pentor slammed the bird on its side and began a max climb out of there just as tracer rounds started to follow us. The gooks were firing by sound. They could not see us but still came pretty close. It looked like they were shooting glowing 55-gallon drums at us!

The recon ream leader radioed, "Sorry, Chatterbox Six, I don't know where these guys came from. We have to move now—we got VC all over the place. We'll contact you when we're clear."

We climbed, and the FAC had us circle around until we started running low on fuel. We were told to RTB (return to base) for fuel and Chatterbox 2, the alternate standby helicopter, took over for us. We fueled up and returned to standby.

About an hour after we returned to standby, we got a call to relieve Chatterbox 2. We took off and returned to the recon team location to wait for further instructions. The FAC said the team had moved about one klick to the east but was in deep trouble. They were flanked on two sides and were fully defensive. They were being attacked by what they thought was about 20 VC.

Once again, the recon team had to run, and they kept this up for about another hour. By this time, it was barely light and the recon team leader radioed, "I'm in deep shit. If you can't get us out in a few minutes, we're fucked! We need CAS [close air support] 100 meters north from my flare now!" A parachute flare was shot off and almost immediately the ground erupted in orange and yellow explosions as one of the A4s made its drop. The recon team leader radioed to the A4 pilot, "You need to drop your next load about 50 meters south of your last drop and you'll have them."

We've all seen the movie where the soldier on the ground calls a strike directly on his own position. This was that movie. This was some scary shit! The second A4 radioed, "Black Bart, get your head down," made his run, dropped his ordnance, and there were more explosions on the ground.

"Hunter, Black Bart. Thanks, Hunter, you got their attention. Good drop."

"Chatterbox Six, Black Bart, the zone is clear. Turn right from your present heading. We're about 25 meters from that last drop. The zone is flat but with tall grass. I'll ident on your call."

By this time, it was light enough to see and Maj. Pentor began his approach.

"Black Bart, Chatterbox Six, pop smoke now."

"Roger."

"Black Bart, copy purple smoke."

"Roger, Chatterbox, confirm purple."

Maj. Pentor went in very hot, flared at the last second, and set the plane down. We immediately came under heavy enemy fire. Muzzle flashes and tracers erupted from everywhere. *Thwack-thwack!* We were taking hits. Even with all the noise and vibration from the helicopter, we could still feel every bullet that hit the bird.

Both the port gunner and I started firing into the jungle at the same time, spraying as large an area as we could. Unbelievably, the intensity of the enemy fire actually increased. *Thwack-thwack-thwack!* More hits. The recon team scrambled on board and the crew chief yelled, "All on board, sir, Go! We're taking fire." *Thwack-thwack-thwack!*

"Sir, we're taking hits!" the crew chief shouted over the deafening noise. It looked like ropes of light coming at us. The fire was that intense. Tracers were lighting the night. This could get really bad. I could feel the bullets hitting our ship and began to move my .50-cal side to side in a spraying motion. The crew chief had a spare belt of ammo ready for me and as my last round ran out, he handed me the lead round in the belt. I jacked the round and continued firing. I never took my thumbs off the triggers. The crew chief helped the port gunner with more ammo and he continued to spray the jungle from his side.

19. Extracting a Recon Team—When Every Second Counts

This was not good. The recon team had started firing their weapons and there was a pretty good outgoing fusillade. Maj. Pentor had exited the zone at no more than 10 feet off the ground and stayed low for about half a mile before climbing. Then, over my flight helmet headset the pilot ordered, "Sergeant Fortner, get up here now!" I moved into the cockpit and saw the master caution light panel lit up. The pilot said, "The SAS [stability augmentation system] and #2 GEN FAIL, APU ON [auxiliary power unit], ENGINE ANTI-ICE, and #2 FUEL LOW lights are all on. Some of them are flickering."

Avionics Electronics School, please don't fail me now!!!

I said, "Reset the master caution panel and see what happens." He reset the panel and the caution lights came back on and flickered. I said, "Turn on the SAS and use a light grip on the stick and then turn it off and see if the controls are the way they are supposed to be and I'll be right back." I told the crew chief that we needed to drop the access door on engine #1, and he was already back there when I got to him. He and I unfastened the Dzus buttons (one-quarter-turn fastening device), dropped the engine access panel, and did a visual inspection. It seemed okay and I said we ought to check #2 while we were here. It looked okay, too. We proceeded to look for hydraulic leaks and found none.

I ran back to the cockpit and looked at the master caution lights and they hadn't changed. "Sir, I don't think there is anything wrong with either engine and we can't find any hydraulic leak. Don't worry about the ENGINE ANTI-ICE light! We probably took some hits to the wiring looms—ignore the lights for now. What happened when you cycled the SAS?"

The pilot said everything seemed okay.

I said, "We know the APU isn't on and I think the number two generator is okay."

Over the radio we heard the FAC calling an air strike on the LZ and a flight of two F4s made a napalm pass that was devastating. Now, three of the six recon team guys were wounded, one of them critically. The recon team guys stripped off his uniform and started to put bandages on him and slow the bleeding. It didn't look good. The recon team leader went to the cockpit and shouted to Maj. Pentor that he needed medical help right now or his man wouldn't make it.

Maj. Pentor asked me, "Why are these goddamn lights on? Did we take any hits in the wiring that you can see?" I ran back to the cabin and found that several of the wire bundles had taken hits. I relayed this to Maj. Pentor and told him I thought we would be okay. He answered, "Well, we're going to the *Sanctuary* [the U.S. hospital ship] and I do not, repeat, *do not* want to get my feet wet."

We were about equidistant from C-Med (medical facility) at Quang Tri and the USS *Sanctuary*; Quang Tri was about five minutes closer. The medical facilities on the *Sanctuary* were the best bet and our med-evacs needed the best.

If you can "firewall" a CH-46D Sea Knight Helicopter, Maj. Pentor did it. That fucking helicopter was rattling and shaking and vibrating like crazy. It was making noises I'd never heard before. I expected the thing to fall apart any second. I looked at the crew chief and raised my eyebrows. He just shrugged and hung on with the rest of us.

The crew chief looked aft out the starboard side and radioed, "Sir, we're trailing a mist and I think it's fuel."

That was all we needed—shit!

The fuel level seemed okay and the master caution panel #1 FUEL LOW light wasn't on so we kept going. Maj. Pentor called the *Sanctuary*, told them to be ready, and relayed the condition of the wounded Marine. He also told them to be ready with fire equipment and that we had a fuel leak of undetermined severity. We approached the *Sanctuary* and Maj. Pentor stood the plane on its tail and dropped to the deck. The rear ramp was already down and two of the recon team members carried the wounded Marine to a waiting gurney on the deck of the ship. He was immediately rushed inside. The other two wounded Marines walked to the waiting doctors. The crew chief and I went out onto the deck and inspected the starboard stub wing and found one bullet hole and leaking fuel. The CH-46 had self-sealing fuel cells and while they were leaking from the bullet hole, the leak wasn't terrible. We stuck rags in the hole.

There were a few other bullet holes on the starboard side just aft of my gun position. About two feet to my right, in fact. That was plenty close enough!

We were only about 15 minutes from base, so we advised the pilot that if he thought we had enough fuel to go ahead and go for it. We also told Maj. Pentor we didn't think the thing would blow up. He repeated his earlier comment, "I still don't want to get my feet wet, so you guys better be right or I'm gonna get really pissed!" We waited a few minutes for the first two Recon guys to get back on and left for Quang Tri.

The major called Quang Tri and told the fire crews to be ready. We landed on the taxiway and shut down. After landing, the Recon guys told us what had happened, and it was the scariest story I'd heard the entire time I was in country.

They'd been in the bush for about six days and came upon a platoon-sized group of NVA soldiers. They followed the NVA for two days and kept track of their activities. Along the way, the recon team discovered numerous places the NVA had supplies hidden. They also found that the route taken south was a new one.

One of the team triggered a hand grenade booby trap and they were dis-

19. Extracting a Recon Team—When Every Second Counts

covered. That started a run through the jungle and there was a lot of close-in fighting. The recon team was able to keep moving but because of the injured man, they were pretty slow. They stopped to rest and got flanked and then the close-in fighting was nearly hand-to-hand. The Recon Leader could actually see the faces of the NVA. Grenades were exchanged and they were so close, they were yelling at the NVA and the NVA were yelling back.

The recon team was able to call for an evac and kept moving until we were able to get them out. The team leader said that if the last air strike hadn't hit where it did, they would all be dead.

We got out of the helicopter and walked around looking for damage. There was only the one bullet hole in the starboard stub wing and a little bit of fuel leaking out. The rotor blades had a few bullet holes in them. Those were neat holes because they were sort of oval instead of round. This was because the blades were moving, and as the bullet passed through the blade, the hole got elongated. We'd already noticed the bullet holes on the starboard side by my gun position.

I walked around to the front of the bird and what I saw scared the shit out of me. I ran back into the cockpit and looked at the ceiling and circuit breaker panel: exit bullet hole. I went back out to the front of the aircraft and called to Maj. Pentor, "Uh, major, you might want to see this." The major came to the front and I pointed out an entry bullet hole on the right front near the clear plastic below the pilot's seat (unlike most other aircraft, the CH-46 had the pilot on the right-hand side and the co-pilot on the left). If you traced the angle of the entry and exit, the path went right through where Maj. Pentor was sitting.

Maj. Pentor looked at the bullet hole. He didn't say a word. He stood there looking for about 30 seconds and walked away.

There are some things that aren't explainable—this was one of those things.

There was no possible way that bullet could have missed him. But it did.

* * *

Enemy body counts were always a subject for discussion during the Vietnam War because it was felt the body counts were inflated so that it would appear the United States was doing better than it really was.

We were later told that the body count for the napalm strike was 42 enemy KIA.

I hoped that number was accurate. I wished it had been more.

The wounded Marine we took to the USS *Sanctuary* died that day.

Damn!

20

Is My Luck About to Run Out?

After six months in-country, guys became eligible for some much-needed R&R. There was an impressive list of places you could go—Tokyo, Hong Kong, Hawaii, the Philippines, Bangkok, and so on. The transportation was free—all you had to do was cover your expenses while there. Lots of guys went to Hong Kong or Bangkok because it was cheap, and getting laid was even cheaper. Some guys went to Tokyo, got laid, and bought stereos. Some guys went to the Philippines and because it was *really* cheap, got laid, and then got laid again. Some guys went to meet their wives or girlfriends in Hawaii (and, well, you get the idea).

Meanwhile, I was starting to get the feeling a lot of guys get in a war zone. I thought that maybe, just maybe, I was going to get killed. It wasn't a horrible or nagging feeling, but just sort of there at the back of my mind. I knew that I was fortunate in being stationed at a reasonably secure base, and my flight missions were generally pretty tame. Even so, I was still in a war zone in the middle of a war, and when my flight missions called me into an enemy action mission, things changed pretty quickly. I felt that because I was flying as air crew and we were going places where we were getting shot at, and some of our squadron's helicopters had been shot down or had crashed and guys were getting dead, I was tempting the law of averages. But, at the same time, I was going to continue flying. I enjoyed the rush I got from flying into dangerous situations.

Because I'd been such a total asshole while I was in high school (an understatement!) and because I'd been so terrible to my family and specifically to my mother, I decided to put in for R&R in Hawaii and have her meet me there. We could enjoy some sightseeing, some fun tourist stuff, and if I got dead later on, at least my mother would have seen me one last time and would have some positive memories of our time together.

I put in for Hawaii and was granted R&R there. Then I called my mother, gave her the dates and got ready to go. I hopped a flight to Danang and got

20. Is My Luck About to Run Out?

processed for a trip out of the country. There were some "do's and don'ts" while on R&R, including not committing a crime, staying in the place where your orders were for, making sure you made it back to Vietnam on time. Mike Ballard from my shop was also going on R&R to Hawaii so we hooked up for the trip. Mike planned to meet his girlfriend there and we decided to all get together and have a good time.

After the processing was complete, we were getting ready to get on a military-chartered PanAm fight when the ammo dump at Danang blew up. This was a huge disaster. There was so much stuff exploding and making so much noise that you had to shout to hear one another. I learned later that it wasn't enemy activity that caused it but something like a lit cigarette or electrical short or something. Nonetheless, it blew up big time!

A large group of people, including Mike and me, were caught out in the open and ran to some revetments on the flight line for cover. We waited there for hours while explosion after explosion rocked us. The concussions and shock waves of the exploding ordnance and ammunition were beyond description!

After four or five hours, the explosions died down a little, and it was deemed safe to board our flight. I was leaving Vietnam for the first time in six months. It was an incredible feeling watching the ground drop away knowing I had a week to get away from that place. After a stop in Okinawa, we flew into

Tim at .50-cal portside, November 1968 (Tim Fortner Collection, Vietnam Center and Archive, Texas Tech University).

Honolulu and were bused to the U.S. Navy R&R Welcoming Center. This was where families and wives could meet the guys coming in.

At the welcoming center, Mike spotted his girlfriend immediately—and she was hard to miss. Kara was absolutely beautiful. Mike grabbed her, hugged her, and just about screwed her on the spot. Kara didn't seem to mind. Mike said, "See ya," and they were in a cab to the hotel.

Meanwhile, I met my mom and we went to the Hilton, where we finally had the chance to talk, just the two of us. She had seemed surprised when I first asked her to spend my R&R with me in Hawaii, but now that we were together, she seemed very happy to see me. I really felt like, after so many years of struggle, we were finally growing closer and putting our past differences behind us. Vietnam had matured me; there was no doubt about that.

Once we were settled in the hotel, I sacked out in my room for about 12 hours and when I woke up, I called Mom and said I needed a drink. The drinking age in Hawaii at the time was 20 years old and I just qualified. It wouldn't have made any difference, anyway.

We met up with Mike and Kara for drinks. They both looked a little worn out, but they were smiling. We began drinking at Davy Jones' Locker beneath the Outrigger Hotel. We drank Mai Tais forever and everyone got smashed. There may have been a luau in there somewhere but I don't remember for sure. I do remember Mike and Kara kissing and hugging and playing grab-ass until finally they disappeared. All that shit was making me even hornier than I already was.

When we all sobered up the next day, my mother said that "such & such" in Santa Cruz said to say hi and that "what's her name" from school wanted me to call her when I got back to the United States. I got to thinking about that and said, "Why don't we go to the airport and get on a United flight to San Francisco? I'll spend a few days at home and then we'll fly back and spend the last two or three days here before I have to go back."

Of course, this was totally illegal and the military would have thrown me in jail if I got caught in San Francisco. This was for good reason—the military knew that if a guy were to go home during his tour in Vietnam, he might, understandably, decide not to go back.

But we opted to take a chance anyway and go for it. We took the United flight to San Francisco and when we arrived, my mom got her car out of long-term parking and off we drove to Santa Cruz. I found "what's her name" and did what any horny, red-blooded, 20-year-old American male would do, and I felt much better. Then I did it again, for good measure.

I spent two days at home, most of that with "what's her name," and we flew back to Hawaii. We hadn't checked out of our rooms so nobody was the wiser. I knew I shouldn't have done it, but I was very glad I did.

I spent the rest of the R&R with my mom and it went really well. The more time we spent together, the easier it was for both of us to just stay in the moment and enjoy each other's company. There was also lots of drinking and eating and general relaxing going on. Mike and Kara kept doing their thing, but we did manage to get together during their breaks. If she wasn't pregnant after that trip, it was a miracle!

The night came when it was time to leave and there were a few tears and all that stuff. Kara wasn't taking her lover's departure well at all and it was decided that after Mike and I left, my mother and Kara would share the same room and console each other.

Mike and I left in a cab for the airport and boarded the PanAm flight. About 10 minutes after takeoff, there was a muffled "bang" and we could feel the plane slow down a little. The pilot came over the PA and said, "We've lost an engine and are returning to Honolulu for repairs. We've still got three good engines, so relax."

Relax? Sure!

We turned around and landed at the airport.

Great!

In the waiting lounge, a Navy guy came in and said it would be at least 10 hours before our plane could get fixed or PanAm could come up with another 707. He also said that we were required to remain at the airport. Mike said, "Fuck that," got on a pay phone to the Hilton and called my mom's room. He talked to Kara and told her to be ready and that he was coming back. We hopped a cab to the Hilton and my buddy and his girlfriend went to their room and closed the door behind them.

It was early in the morning and the bars were closed, but my mom had some vodka and the hotel had orange juice, so we drank screwdrivers for the next six hours. I called Mike in the next room and told him we'd better get going and we left for the airport again. Mike could barely walk, so I assumed he had made the most of our delay.

Go, Mike!

We took off again and this time our flight was uneventful. We made a stop in Okinawa, and before we knew it, we were landing at Danang. I caught a hop to Quang Tri and returned to duty. *Only six more months, I told myself, and the next flight home will be for good.*

I still had that nagging thought, though, at the back of my mind, that I might not make it out alive. I just couldn't shake it, no matter how hard I tried.

* * *

On February 21, 1969, I was assigned to a two-ship CH-46D med-evac standby flight located at the Charlie Med pad at Vandegrift Combat Base. We had a Navy corpsman with us that day. It was daytime and we were sitting around the bird reading and eating C-rats when Maj. Matheson overheard a call that there were several med-evacs on Route #9 between Cam Lo and the Rockpile. Maj. Matheson launched prior to receiving clearance or a briefing. He later received clearance to proceed, but his early launch likely saved several lives.

When we reached the area, our wingman flew cover and Maj. Matheson began an approach from the south. There were at least two overturned jeeps on the road, guys lying in the road, and a bunch of blown-up, twisted stuff that was unrecognizable. There were several wounded or dead Marines on the ground and about 15 Marines who had set up a loose perimeter. To the port side there was about 15 feet of cleared area before a short tree line. On my side (starboard) there was about 75 feet of more or less clear area before some brush and then dense jungle.

We set the bird down and the corpsman and crew chief left to assist with bringing aboard the stretchers with the wounded. While this was going on, we began taking enemy fire from the port side. The port gunner, Cpl. Robb, opened up with his .50-cal. At the same time, our wingman's gunner overhead opened up and started delivering fire on the same side. My side was fine and there was no fire coming from that direction.

Once all the wounded were aboard, we began to lift off. Suddenly enemy fire erupted from the jungle on my side of the aircraft. We were about five feet off the ground when out of the jungle came tracers and muzzle flashes. The air was thick with incoming bullets. I began returning fire, as did the crew chief and corpsman. There was one area where the muzzle flashes and tracers were really visible, and I concentrated on that spot. I did an occasional sweep but directed my fire to that one concentration of incoming fire. I silenced that area with short .50-cal bursts.

Cpl. Robb kept on firing at his gooks and our wingman shot at everything we didn't. More tracers started coming at my side of the aircraft, slightly to the south of the now-silenced position. I directed my fire toward those tracers and quickly shut down that attack position.

There were no more live NVA there. And if anyone had somehow survived my .50-cal fire, they weren't in good shape.

A flight of two gunships showed up and started to blow up the jungle around where the enemy fire was coming from on both sides of the road. I used up my box of ammo and changed to another and kept on firing at the fuckers anyway until we were out of the area.

Amazingly, no bullets hit our bird. I've never understood why. There was a literal wall of tracer rounds going both ways by our bird and we didn't take a hit. Hard to believe.

We headed to the 3rd Medical Battalion at Quang Tri and off-loaded our wounded. I don't think any of the wounded Marines died, even though two of

20. Is My Luck About to Run Out?

them were seriously fucked up. I truly believe that the heroic actions of Maj. Matheson saved their lives that day.

After that flight, we returned to Vandegrift to continue on med-evac standby. For the rest of the day, we cleaned shell casings and blood off the floor of our bird. It was a fucked-up job. If you haven't seen something like that before, it leaves an impression that lasts forever. It's still hard for me to believe that a human body can lose so much blood and still survive. We wiped up what we could and then got a water buffalo (water tank on wheels) and hose and just washed everything out.

I remember looking at those guys on the floor and on stretchers and thinking that this shit not only could really happen, it *was* really happening. You could get hurt and killed and that would be the end of everything. From that day onward, I've had a different attitude and outlook about death and dying. I became harder and more callous about dying.

Missions like this one occurred several times, and I would look at the wounded guys bleeding or the guys who were dead and think, "I'm still alive. I'm sorry you are hurt or dead, but I'm happy that I am okay."

It's not that I didn't feel emotion about their plight; I did, and still do. Seeing guys shot up or with their guts or brains hanging out makes you sick. I always felt bad, and my heart hurt for those wounded we med-evac'ed. It was just that somebody was going to die in this place and I didn't want it to be me. I found I had to look at the wounded and dying Marines with a sense of detachment. I had to; that was the only way I could survive emotionally and psychologically.

But when I looked at dead VC or NVA (not often but on a few occasions), I thought, "Good, you fucks! I'm glad you're dead," and felt absolutely nothing for them.

We later learned that the small convoy was heading down Route 9 and one of the jeeps hit a mine. The other jeep was hit by a command-detonated mine toward the rear of the convoy. The convoy encountered no enemy fire and called for a med-evac. The enemy had set up an ambush to see if it could shoot down a couple of our rescue helicopters as we came in for the med-evac. The gooks waited until just prior to our leaving the zone to open fire on us. Crafty little fuckers.

I'm convinced that the fire returned by our bird and our wingman's bird fucked them up a lot. Our fire was deadly accurate. Those NVA were dead. I know that the gunships pounded the NVA firing positions after we departed the area, further decimating the ambush positions.

What was amazing about that particular mission was that the entire air crew functioned as a unit. Everyone did his job and there was no panic. Even in the face of real danger, everybody just kept his poise. I don't know how Maj. Matheson could hold his helicopter on the ground and wait patiently (and professionally), but he did. I think that there is something to be said for our training—it worked, and thereby saved numerous lives.

My work in the avionics shop limited my flight time. While I did not fly as many missions as the pilots or crew chiefs, I flew enough. It's what I wanted to do. If I could have flown every day, I would have. I wanted to do my job flying and eliminate the opposition while assisting our Marines (and sometimes Army brothers) with resupplies and any other assistance I could offer. But one thought still remained at the back of my mind: How much longer did I have if I kept flying? How long before my own luck might run out?

21

Boosting a Jeep from the Military Police

I was about three-quarters of the way through my time in Vietnam when my slot for an in-country R&R came up. The military had a few places for in-country R&R where guys could get away from the war—places like Vung Tau, Danang, or Saigon. Vung Tau was probably okay; there was a beach there and some stuff set up for creature comforts, but it was mainly Army guys and a long way south. Danang was a big city that was mainly for REMFs and a place to get laid and get the clap for not a lot of money. Saigon, on the other hand, was a place to get into real trouble. Given that I was in Vietnam, which wasn't the fun capital of the world, and I didn't give a shit about the R&R spots on offer, I decided to try to get down to Chu Lai and see Rusty before he went home from Vietnam. I wanted to make sure we saw each other one last time, just in case something bad happened or I got dead before my tour ended.

I got on one of our birds doing a supply pick-up and headed to Danang, and from there I hopped on a Huey headed for Chu Lai. I had managed to contact Rusty in advance and he was waiting for me at Chu Lai Air Base when I landed. We went through the normal BS of hugging and saying how glad we were to see each other and all that shit. Rusty was with the Crash Crew & Air Rescue gang at Chu Lai and they had their own hooch. This place was nice compared to the digs I was used to. It would be like a grunt coming in from the boonies to an enclosed building with beds.

The Crash Crew hooch was a type of Quonset hut complete with running AC (still no flush toilets, though). These guys put me up in a bunk and we sat down to a world record marathon game of "back-alley bridge." I don't remember how the game was played but I do remember that it was fun and we played for hours.

Then it came time for some serious drinking. Well, it would have been serious except for the fact that the only thing the crash crew guys had was some obscure brand of really shitty gin, some old Carling Black Label beer in "tin" cans (rusting tin with formaldehyde as a preservative) and some ginger ale.

Tim's friend Rusty enjoying himself while on crash-crew duty at the front of a plane that has just gone off the runway, August 1969 (Tim Fortner Collection, Vietnam Center and Archive, Texas Tech University).

Barf!

I had a secret stash with me, but that was for Rusty and me later on.

So here I was, drinking gin-and-ginger ale and playing back-alley bridge when suddenly, *kaboom!* An explosion that was fairly close and had some concussion. All the crash crew guys just about killed each other getting out of the hooch and into the bunker while I sat there and listened to a few more bangs and walked outside to see what the noise was all about. The base was getting rocketed but the rounds were landing pretty far from where I was, so I just watched the show. There were guys from around the base running and hollering and jumping into holes and bunkers and under jeeps.

When stuff quieted down and people were crawling out from wherever it was they had fled to, they started asking why I never came into the bunker.

21. Boosting a Jeep from the Military Police

I explained that in Quang Tri, we didn't go into the bunkers unless the rockets were landing close enough to be really worrisome (which, fortunately, didn't happen very often), and that most of the time we would climb up on top of our hooch to watch the show. Also, our bunkers were prone to have water in them and sometimes even snakes, so we always figured it was better to take our chances on the outside unless we were getting something like direct hits.

As it turned out, Chu Lai got rocketed a few more times that night and by about three or four a.m., we were all pretty fucked up and nobody bothered to run for cover anymore.

Rusty had to go with his crash crew bunch the next day, poor fucker. Everybody was hung over and I was no exception—what a fucking headache! I slept in, got up, and went back to sleep. Rusty went to work. He dragged in at the end of his shift, grabbed a shower, knocked back a few gin-and-ginger ales and started feeling better.

I'd had enough of the local drink, so we all decided to hit the NCO enlisted club and have a beer. The Marine Corps, in its infinite wisdom, had decided that officers in the Marine Corps had an Officer's Club and that club served hard liquor. The Marine Corps must have felt the officers were more responsible and could drink hard liquor without consequence. Probably a correct assumption.

The enlisted men had the Enlisted Club and there you could get either beer or beer. At least that was how it was at Quang Tri and Chu Lai. If you have never had Carling Black Label or Brew 102, brewed with formaldehyde (as a preservative) that has been put into a tin can and left out in the sun on a pallet for eight months, you haven't experienced really shitty beer or the worst hangover. I mean the shit the Marine Corps had for its enlisted men to drink was worse than shameful.

Semper Fi!

After half a dozen of these brews and a little shitty bar food, it really didn't make much difference—booze was booze and eventually it had the desired effect.

A lot of enlisted clubs in Vietnam had entertainment—or what passed for entertainment. The Chu Lai E-club was no exception. Chu Lai had a Vietnamese "band" fielding three guys with a "girl" singer about 45 years old (face paint, a few teeth, tube top, hot pants), complete with two really old electric guitars and a clapped-out set of drums. This group had a repertoire of songs including favorites from the Beatles and the Beach Boys and Sonny and Cher. If you have never heard "Puppy Ruv" or "Sroop John B," or "I Got Chu, Babe," or a medley of Elvis songs ... sung in pidgin English by a group of Vietnamese, after a bunch of Carling Black Label beers and after eating bar food of unknown origin, you haven't lived.

Girl singer started looking good, too!

Fuck it—time to go. It was late and we were major-league fucked up. The walk to the club wasn't far but the walk back seemed like a long haul, in our condition. Rusty and I walked for a while and he leaned against a parked jeep and—yep, you guessed it! The conversation went something like this:

"Hey, let's steal the fucker and ride back."

"Sounds good—where's the key?"

"Don't need a key. Watch this."

"Yeah, you need a key."

"Do not."

"Okay, numb-nuts, how you gonna start it?"

"Watch this."

And, drunk as he was, Rusty pulled the spade terminal wires off the back of the ignition switch, hooked them together, pressed the starter button, and the jeep started.

Good goin', Russ!

"Learned that when we had to get a license to drive these things. Instructor said the keys to these fuckers were always getting lost and if you needed a jeep, this was the way."

Hey, better-larceny-and-theft courses offered by the USMC. Right on!

I hopped in and off we went, roughly in the direction of the Crash Crew Hooch. About an hour or so later (this was only about a half-mile trip) we ended up pretty close to the hooch, were a bit more sober, and the fucking jeep stopped. The next brilliant conversation went like this.

"Why'd you shut it off?"

"Didn't. Just quit."

"Start it up."

"Won't start."

"Why not?"

"Don't know."

"Fuck it; we're almost there anyway. Let's walk."

We dismounted and walked around the front of the jeep. That was when the words "Military Police" stenciled on the front of the jeep caught my eye.

Oh shit!

Well, if you're going to boost a jeep, you might as well boost a cop's jeep. We stumbled the rest of the way to the hooch and passed out.

The next morning, we were really badly hung over. This was a first-class, world-record fucking hangover. Rusty had to go to work and I decided to go with him. It was my last day of in-country R&R. Rusty talked to his CO and got me cleared to ride in the crash truck for the day while Rusty was stationed out on the runway watching airplanes land.

One longtime tradition in the United States Marine Corps was a "Short Timer's Ribbon" worn in the vent holes of a utility cap or the band of a hel-

21. Boosting a Jeep from the Military Police

met. The ribbon signified the wearer to be "short," meaning that the lucky wearer had less than 30 days left "in-country." This was a badge coveted by all. A "30-day badge" told everyone that you were going home!

Now, as it happened that day, I had stashed a bottle of Seagram's 7 in my bag when I came to Chu Lai to see Rusty. A Seagram's 7 bottle is sealed with a quarter-inch-wide black and yellow ribbon: a "Short Timer's Ribbon." The tradition is to open the bottle, put the ribbon on your hat, and drink the contents.

So here we were, parked at the tail end of the runway at Chu Lai. There were three of us: Rusty, me, and a corporal named Johnny Walder. Rusty was in charge of the crash crew truck and we were on active crash duty; it's a hundred million degrees, and the humidity is off the charts. Perfect time to pop out the Seagram's 7. Rusty had just gone under 30 days left in country and I presented the bottle to him, gave him a hug, and told him to pull off the ribbon and open the bottle. Rusty tied the ribbon in the vent holes in his cap and we drank the stuff straight out of the bottle.

Keep in mind that we are sitting on a very active runway with planes taking off and landing every few minutes (or even more frequently). A-4s, C-130s, C-123s, F-4s, C-47s, with a few helicopters and some Air America stuff thrown in. A lot of the planes carried bombs and ordnance—which makes sense, considering this was a war zone.

So the bottle cap of the Seagram's 7 is long gone, the ribbon is on Rusty's cap, the bottle is just about empty, we are shirtless and totally drunk. It's about 10:30 in the morning.

Rusty's drifting in and out of a drunken stupor, Walder is passed out in the back seat, and I'm only half conscious. If the F-4 Phantoms and A-4s hadn't been taking off with noise that could wake the dead, all three of us would have been out cold.

Out of the corner of my one, barely open, eye, I watched a C-123 land and reverse the props—except that one of the props did not reverse.

Oh shit!

I banged on Rusty's arm and started yelling, and Rusty woke up and saw this happening, and the plane hung a hard right off the runway and into the sand and came right at the truck.

Oh shit!

To his credit, Rusty fired the crash truck up, slammed it into reverse, and backed away from the oncoming plane. The plane came to a stop, and Rusty and Walder fell out of the truck onto the sand and dragged themselves up. I had another shot from what was left in the bottle while staying within the safe confines of the truck. Rusty grabbed a hose and he and Walder did some crash crew fire-fighting shit.

About that time, the right-hand door of the plane opened and the crew chief came running out and ran right past us yelling, "Get away—10,000 pounds of dynamite!" The pilot and co-pilot followed shortly, each running in a different direction.

Oh shit!

Rusty, drunker than a fucking skunk, walked up to the plane and went inside. Out he came and let us know it was all okay; nothing was on fire and nothing was going to blow us to hell. Rusty got on the radio in the truck and said something like "Crush Crew 47 inch-ident on runway 180 ish code something [under control]. Need mule for tow and a few shees of Marsell matting." *Burp.*

The next thing I saw was about 10 crash trucks heading our way being led by a jeep with an officer. From my first day in Chu Lai, I recognized the major as Rusty's CO.

Oh shit. Leavenworth, here we come!

This whole convoy set up a perimeter, guys with fire hoses were all over the place, and Rusty was standing at the nose of the plane looking at the buried nose gear. I shouted at Russ to smile and then took a quick picture and slinked off behind another crash truck. As the CO was walking up to Rusty, I was hitching a ride back to the operations building on another crash truck.

Time to scram!

On the runway in front of the operations building sat ET4, a helicopter from my squadron in Quang Tri. I hopped inside and asked if I could hitch a ride back to Quang Tri and beat-feet it out of there.

Somehow, amazingly, Rusty didn't get busted and didn't get thrown in the brig after this little adventure. The CO gave him a reprimand and made him work some extra hours and do some menial bullshit, but nothing went into his official record and he pretty much skated around disaster. He told me later (much later) that the CO was from Monterey and that they knew a few of the same people in civilian life. The CO was getting short, too, and must have taken pity on Rusty. My name never came up (thanks, Russ!), and I managed to get out of that deal unscathed.

Rusty was going home. But I was still left wondering how much longer I would survive, and if I, like Rusty, would ever have that chance to go home.

22

Seven Lives Gone

The Marine side of Quang Tri Air Base was set up with the Thach Han River on one side, and on the other side, a long row of shops, hangars, and admin buildings, then the flight line and aircraft parking area, and finally the active runway. All of the HMM 262, HMM 161, and VMO-6 aircraft were parked in what were called "revetments." The revetments were 10 feet high by about four to five feet wide. They were built with thick-ribbed steel and filled with sand. Imagine a tall shoebox open at the top and you get the idea. The revetments were placed side by side and the spacing was wide enough and long enough to park our helicopters or OV-10 ("ohveebashten") Broncos or Hueys and the like. The revetments served as protection against a rocket or mortar attack. And they worked.

On several occasions our base would take incoming in the form of rockets (rarely mortars) aimed at the flight line. The revetments protected the aircraft by acting as shields to explosions and the subsequent shrapnel from the explosions. Our helicopters or HMM-161's didn't carry any ordnance or bombs or rockets—just internal guns. VMO-6 had UH1Es (Hueys) and OV-10 Broncos. Both aircraft carried external rocket pods.

One day there was a big whoosh followed shortly by a big explosion—*whoosh, bang!*

I was working in the Avionics shop with the rest of our guys and we thought it was a rocket attack. We all hauled ass to the bunker and waited until it had been quiet for a few minutes and then wandered out to the flight line to see what had happened.

We found that one of the revetments had a large hole in it, end-on, and smoke was coming from the revetment wall. About 200 feet down the flight line was a UH1E with the left-hand rocket pod smoking slightly and a guy standing beside the pod. He was looking down, shaking his head, and then looking at the hole in the revetment and back again.

We went over to him and learned that he was an Avionics guy from VMO-6. The Huey had a yellow sheet gripe (a form for aircraft that alerts maintenance to any problems) that the left-hand rocket pod hadn't fired when the aircraft was on rocket run. There are procedures in place to prevent any type of accidental discharge or firing of ordnance. So this had to be the perfect storm of fuck-ups.

When any aircraft carrying ordnance lands, it's required to taxi to the ordnance area of the field. There, the crew or the ordnance guys "safe" and de-arm any rockets or bombs and put "REMOVE BEFORE FLIGHT" flags in the safetied areas. Normally, the pilots pull the circuit breakers to the firing system and the crew chief checks everybody's work. When there is an electrical issue with a firing system and rockets are involved, there are additional and stringent procedures to follow. You need to make sure that the circuit breakers are pulled, that the firing switch armament safety covers are in the down position, that the connecting plugs (Cannon plugs) to the rocket pods are disconnected and safety covers put in place, that there is nothing in front of the rocket pod, that there is a second man standing guard so that nobody can inadvertently reset the circuit breakers, and so on.

And ... you are supposed to unload the rockets from the pod or remove the loaded pod completely. In short, you are supposed to secure the system so that there is no way it can go off.

So this is what happened. When the Huey returned from its mission, the pilots went to the refueling area and refueled, completely bypassing the de-arming area. This was a giant fuck-up! Going into the fuel dump area with live rocket pods was total stupidity. In addition, they had already experienced a problem with the rocket pod not firing so they were aware that there was an issue.

The Avionics guy working on the Huey was fairly new to VMO-6 and was on his own checking out the problem. Apparently, he took a volt/ohm meter and began chasing the electrical system wiring. And he did everything wrong.

He assumed that the pilots had pulled the breakers but never verified that. This wasn't the actual cause of the rocket going off, but contributed to the chain of events. It was a fuck-up nonetheless. For the record, the rocket pod circuit breakers had not been pulled. Strike two for the pilots.

There is a test unit made for the rocket pod and it works pretty well. After you take out all the rockets, you hook up the test unit and chase the problem. Nothing can go wrong because there is nothing to fire or blow up.

The Avionics guy either didn't know the procedures (probable) or was just lazy (possible) and didn't have the test unit with him. On top of that, the rocket pod was still fully loaded! He disconnected the Cannon Plug to the inoperative rocket pod and checked the wiring to the switch side of the plug—it all worked. He reconnected the Cannon Plug, went to the cockpit, and put the leads of the ohmmeter to the rear contacts of the switch.

Whoosh/bang!

22. Seven Lives Gone

The ohmmeter works with an internal 9-volt battery to run current through a wire to see if it has connectivity or a short or has an open circuit. Nine volts to the firing circuit was enough electricity to set the rocket off. Amazingly, only one rocket ignited.

Fortunately, the rocket hit the end of the revetment and did no other damage. Other than a revetment with a hole in it and several thousand dollars' worth of rocket blown up, it was pretty tame compared to what could have happened. Everybody involved in this deal got in some sort of trouble. As they should have. Those rules, guidelines, and safety procedures were in place because of accidents like this. It's actually surprising that this shit didn't happen more often.

* * *

During most of my time in Vietnam, I was stationed at a reasonably secure base. There weren't a whole lot of attacks on our base nor were there ever Viet Cong or NVA at the wire attacking us. There were a few probes at night and there were a few rocket attacks, but generally it was pretty safe. We didn't get shot at while at the base (well, not often). We also did not normally see wounded Marines or KIAs at our base.

Not only was our base relatively safe, most of our flight missions were pretty tame and even boring, to a point. Resupply missions were only occasionally dangerous. Most of the time we flew around and delivered supplies and then went back to the base.

Simple and easy. Most of the time.

Even though most of our missions were safe and routine, there were exceptions, of course, and when it got bad, it got really, really bad. All of us who flew saw a lot of bloody, badly injured guys. Unfortunately, we saw a lot of death, too. It was unavoidable, given the job we were doing. The perception of violence and death, for most people, comes from television and books, not from firsthand experience. I don't think most people could take what really happens firsthand. On television, the policeman shoots the bank robber and the gun goes "pop, pop, pop." The policeman's gun doesn't kick. The bank robber is blown back 10 feet and falls to the pavement. The policeman rushes up to the bank robber and says, "I told you to drop the gun. I didn't want to shoot you."

The bank robber has been shot three times in the chest and has three dots of what looks like ketchup on his shirt. The bank robber says to the cop, "Tell my wife and kids that I loved them. Tell them I'm sorry I robbed banks and shot at people. Tell little Billy I will miss seeing him play the violin. Tell them that I did it because I needed the money to cover my gambling debts. Tell them blah, blah, blah, blah, blah…"

Then the bank robber takes a deep breath, closes his eyes, and dies. Very gentle, very peaceful.

Believe me, it's nothing like that in real life. Not in the least.

But because most people don't know any different, they think how death is portrayed in movies and TV is how it is in real life. But they are so wrong. When somebody gets shot, they fall down (unless they are already on the ground) and they bleed. A lot. If they get shot in the chest, they normally fall down or go immediately into shock. And they bleed. A lot. They don't gesture for the corpsman to come over so they can talk to him for 20 minutes. And the gun that fired the bullets kicked and made a really loud fucking noise when it went off, not a pop. But you'd never understand that just from watching TV. You can only understand that by witnessing it firsthand.

There were times when our flight missions took us into danger and we experienced, firsthand, what wounded and dead people look like. We saw men with wounds so horrible that only a doctor should see them. We saw blood, lots of blood. We saw intestines hanging out of wounded Marines. We saw brains spilling out of skulls of living people. We saw wounded brought aboard who were missing arms or legs or both, with bloody, makeshift bandages on the stumps. We saw blood pouring out of men's mouths.

We watched Marines and Army guys die from their wounds before we could get them medical aid. Most of us there were around 20 years old at the time and saw things that would sicken most people two or three times our age.

What we saw was real. This wasn't CNN. We weren't watching television or a movie. We couldn't leave when it was over. We learned that dead was dead and there was no going back. You have to experience this to fully realize what it is like. It's real. It's final. And it's fucked.

* * *

Near the end of my tour of duty in Vietnam, we seemed to be doing more troop insertions and then later, extractions. I don't know if the United States wanted to make a last push against the VC and NVA or if those operations were planned in advance.

In mid–September 1969, we launched on a troop insertion from Vandy to a location near the DMZ and a little west of Dong Ha. It seemed an unlikely place for an insertion but that really didn't mean anything. We'd done insertions in places that didn't look like much before.

We did our normal staging, picked up the troops, and flew to the LZ. We off-loaded the Marines and went back to Vandy for another load. This occupied most of the day. Just another mission, one of many. Nothing of note and nothing to remember.

About two or three days later, we were flying resupply to the same zone and had an internal load of supplies, mail, and some replacements. Entering the LZ, I could see that bunkers had been built and a perimeter had been established with guards posted.

22. Seven Lives Gone

I also saw body bags.

A body bag is a thick, rubberized plastic bag with a long zipper down the center from top to bottom. It has "D"-type cloth handles on both sides and ends. We'd transported dead bodies in body bags prior to this and it was never a nice experience. It was as grim as it can get. There is such a total finality in it, knowing that inside the bag was someone whose life had just ended.

On this day, I saw seven body bags lined up perfectly, side by side, in one area of the camp. Alongside the body bags were about 10 dead VC in black pajamas. We landed and off-loaded our supplies and the replacement troops. The replacements knew they were replacing the dead men in the body bags.

Seven body bags. Seven dead Marines. Seven dead young men. Seven lives gone.

What a fucking waste.

For that to be the temporary resting place for those guys was tragic.

The Marines at the LZ began loading the body bags on board and we went out to help. There was no ceremony or ritual accompanying this, but we treated those dead with all the respect and care they deserved. We didn't just dump them on the floor of the helicopter.

We placed each man on the floor gently.

It was difficult not to tear up.

When the dead were loaded, the Marines who were helping load the bodies on board left.

One of those Marines walked out of the back of our helicopter and looked down at the row of dead VC. He shook his head and then wiped his eyes with the back of his hand.

Then he took out his .45 pistol and emptied it into the first VC in the row.

We lifted off and transported the dead Marines to Charlie Med at Quang Tri. We unloaded the dead Marines and lined them up perfectly, side by side, with as much care and concern as we could. Prior to taking off from Charlie Med, the crew stood at attention and saluted those fallen heroes, seven brave young men who had just made the ultimate sacrifice for their country.

23

Heading Home

By late 1969, the unpopular war in Vietnam was beginning to wind down. Internal political and external international pressure was making it pretty clear that the United States was going to have to pull out of Vietnam. President Nixon's "Vietnamization Plan" was partially in effect. It may not have been working, but it was in effect.

HMM 262 got orders to begin breaking down the squadron for the purpose of relocation. We were told that the squadron would be sent to Marble Mountain, Danang, to continue operations. The plan, as we were told, was that all remaining Marine helicopter squadrons would be consolidated at Marble Mountain Air Facility (MMAF). Our squadron got orders to begin breaking down the base and pack parts and supplies for shipment south. At first, we shipped items and equipment that wasn't essential to the squadron's operation. As time went on, we began shipping out everything, including our aircraft. The helicopters that could fly were sent to Danang. The birds that could not fly were air-lifted (via giant Sikorsky helicopters for lifting large loads) to freighters and then shipped home. HMM 262 personnel were to follow to Danang.

Several days before we left Quang Tri, a typhoon of enormous magnitude hit and wrecked a lot of stuff: hangars, buildings, hootches, and so on. There was damage to several of our helicopters. It was a mess. There was some pretty severe flooding to the base and it made our departure a huge pain in the ass.

While the typhoon was winding down, our squadron personnel (what was left of it, mainly enlisted) were flown by C-130 to Phu Bai to await transport to Danang. We were supposed to be going to Danang but instead got stuck in Phu Bai.

I have never figured that out. The only thing I can come up with was that there was a drop-dead date for the United States to be out of Quang Tri and they had no choice but to move us out when they did.

I learned much later that at some point in that short time period, orders for HMM 262's relocation were changed from Marble Mountain in Danang

23. Heading Home

Returning stateside after tour of duty. Tim outside his "hiding place" on the USS *Iwo Jima*, October 6, 1969 (Tim Fortner Collection, Vietnam Center and Archive, Texas Tech University).

to Phu Bai! I was getting short and had less than 15 days left in country. I thought we would be in Danang and leave for CONUS (continental United States) from there.

When we got to Phu Bai, it was under water. I'm not talking a little run-off or standing water but a full-blown flood, a remnant of the typhoon.

The C-130 landed and some of the squadron personnel got off. We piled out the rear ramp with our sea bags and other personal items, rifles, and the like onto the Marston Matting.

There was no one on the flight line; in reality, there was no flight line because it was flooded. This was fucked up. Our senior NCO was G/Sgt Abrahms. Abrahms was a really good guy and very well respected by our group. At Quang Tri, he was NCOIC of the AC Hydraulics shop and one very good aircraft mechanic. It fell on him to take charge of our gaggle and get us someplace other than where we were.

We spent three days in Phu Bai before receiving word that HMM 262 was going to be relocated there. There was little or no paperwork for us then, and I needed to find out how to get to Danang for my rotation date.

On the third day, a C-130 landed carrying the squadron paperwork, including the documents I needed. The following day, I boarded a C-130 and flew to Danang. After all that, the trip to Danang took all of 20 minutes.

What a joke!

I off-loaded at Danang and was taken to some barracks by cattle cars (military buses). Danang was bustling with activity and there was a lot of stuff that had been discarded and was just lying by the side of the road. The pullout was causing the United States to dump unnecessary supplies and the locals were having a great time with our discards.

The barracks I got deposited in were close to the harbor and docks. Some REMF enlisted guys and a REMF 2nd lieutenant came to the barracks to process us out for the trip home.

It was a pretty big mess in Danang. Danang was the point of departure for thousands of guys in all branches of the service and the system was way past overloaded. The REMFs did what they could but had to reconstruct who we were and where we'd come from. I had transport orders and it helped a little. It was fucking chaos and disorganized in the extreme. This all took time.

There were so many people in the area that it was tough to get to the mess hall they had temporarily set up for us and for the rest of the people getting sent out. Tempers were short and morale was in the can. Fortunately, my paperwork and orders could be processed so that I would get passage on a Navy ship bound for home.

I was assigned a number on a 3 × 5 index card. No shit! A 3 × 5 card with a number written in ballpoint pen! When they called your number, you were supposed to go get on a cattle car and go wherever it was going. At about 4 p.m. in the afternoon of September 26, 1969, my number was called and I headed to a bus.

At the bus, an REMF Navy asshole with a clipboard told the group I was with to sit by the side of a building and wait for the next bus because this bus was full. When the next cattle car arrived, a line of guys got on and the bus left. This happened several more times, until I got up and went over to the Navy asshole and asked when we were going to get on a bus.

He said something about "fucking Jarheads," and "Marine assholes," and "dumb grunts." He said we had to wait our turn and told me to go sit back down.

I still had my M16 (later turned in to the USMC while in transport). I'd had enough of this guy. I cocked my M16, pointed it at his balls, and told him

23. Heading Home

that if we didn't get on the next bus, I was going to make him a eunuch. I told him I wasn't fucking kidding, that I was having a very bad day, and that if he talked in a high-pitched voice for the rest of his life, I didn't much give a shit. He turned green and started shaking.

Good!

At that same time, this Navy asshole got relieved (his lucky day) by another Navy guy. I explained to the new guy what had happened to us. He told me to wait a second and that he would find out what had happened. At least this guy gave a shit and found out that we should have been long gone. It was about midnight by this point and we got on the next bus out.

Finally.

As it turned out, that delay getting on a bus to the harbor turned out to be a very good thing. The bus headed to the harbor and pulled up alongside a clapped-out, rusty, paint-peeling, listing, round-bottomed, dented hunk of shit that the Navy called a boat. The fucking thing looked like it was sinking and it was still tied to a goddamn dock!

Oh shit!

This piece of crap was the pride of the fucking Navy—the USS *Bexar*, nicknamed the "USS *Bear*."

I was sure I was fucked.

Somebody told us to get off the bus, head up a gangplank, get on the USS *Bear*, and show our number to somebody on the boat. My squadron mates and I laid back a little to see what was going to happen and let the majority of the people on the bus go up the gangplank before us. If there was a way for me to not get on that piece of crap, I was going to attempt it.

The guy who was about the 50th to go up the plank got turned around, came down, and told us, "They said the boat is overfull and we are supposed to go back to where we came from and get assigned another boat."

Jesus. What a mess.

About 500 feet from the USS *Bear* sat the LPH USS *Iwo Jima* and on deck were Marine CH-34s and CH-46s. The three Marines in my group and I got the same idea all at once, slinked off into the shadows, and headed for the *Iwo Jima*. By this time, it was about two or three a.m. and we were beat. Behind us the rust-bucket USS *Bear* was being pulled out by a tug.

Bold as we could be and with nothing to lose, we walked up the gangplank of the *Iwo Jima*. At the top was a lieutenant (Jg) with a clipboard. I walked up to him, saluted, and said, "Sir, we were told by the Navy captain on the USS *Bear* that we'd been assigned to your ship for transport, Sir. They gave us these numbers to give to the Officer of the Deck, Sir. They said if there were any questions to give them a call." Then we waited.

The lieutenant replied, "We're pretty full too, but grab one of those cots and see the ensign over there." The ensign looked at us and said something to the effect that the boat was full and that all the crew and sleeping areas were full and that he didn't know where to put us. He said that for tonight only there was an unused refueling area on the flight deck that we could bunk in. He said we could sort out the paperwork in the morning, after we pulled out of Danang Harbor.

He led us up some stairs and down some stairs and outside and inside and we were totally lost. We went through a door and onto the flight deck and to a door that opened to a room about 10 feet square with a clean linoleum floor and an outer door. The door opened to a catwalk at the outside of the ship and a deck next to the ocean. *Hmmm.* The ensign said he was sorry it was cramped but we could get it sorted out in the morning.

The four of us set up camp in the refueling room and the next morning we went in search of food. What we found was frightening, and we discussed our course of action for the next month.

There were lines of Marines everywhere. They all had paperwork in their hands. Other Marines were getting PT (physical training) on the flight deck by some hard-assed drill sergeant types. Still others were in lines to get shots and physicals and stuff. More guys were lined up getting numbers for when they could get showers. On top of that, the ship was so full that the sleeping quarters were rotated so that while some people were awake and doing PT, or labor, or cleaning the heads, or some other horrible shit, the other shift would sleep. Then the shifts would reverse.

Fuck that!

We beat a hasty retreat to the refueling room and had a meeting. So far, no one had found us or knew where we were. The window to the flight deck and the window in the door could be covered so that no one could see in. They got covered in a hurry! We figured that with so many people on the ship, we could probably go unnoticed for a while and avoid all the shit details. We thought that if we moved about the ship in ones or twos, we had a good chance of going undetected. We sent out scouts to get the lay of the land.

We learned that the ship laundry would take your clothes and return them clean with no questions. We found that when the call for the chow hall came (also in rotation) that we could easily blend into a line of people waiting to get fed and then disappear after eating. Showers were a little more difficult because water was rationed and they kept a close eye on that. We got around that by getting into the line of guys leaving the shower and then walking into the shower from the exits—nobody checked anybody leaving. We only showered every two or three days or so to stay under the radar.

The *Iwo Jima* had a ship's store that was fantastic. All the cigarettes, junk food, and candy you wanted plus a current selection of magazines and books. We stocked up and sat back to enjoy the trip.

We were cruising pleasantly on the *Iwo Jima* and avoiding all the Marine

Corps bullshit. No PT, no calisthenics, no work details, no nothing. We sat in the refueling room, kept very quiet, ate junk food, read books, smoked, and enjoyed our deck to the ocean. All in all, a pleasant voyage.

We docked in Okinawa for resupply and on the other dock sat the "Pride of the United States Navy," the USS *Bear*. The ships were docked side-on with a pier in between. We were maybe 100 feet apart. The supplies began to be loaded on board each ship and we slunk off to our stateroom to avoid detection and forced labor. A lot of food was being loaded on board and along with it, lots and lots of citrus.

We were watching the *Bear* from our stateroom when an orange flew out from the rust-bucket troop ship to the *Iwo*.

Then another. And another.

Then an orange was lobbed from the *Iwo* to the *Bear*.

What happened next was pretty unbelievable. The biggest food fight in both naval and Marine Corps history commenced. There were times when you couldn't see across the pier because there was so much food in the air. The *Bear* looked like it had been in a paintball fight. You couldn't see the pier's surface because of all the food.

The officers on both ships attempted to break up the food fight, but each time an officer would show his face, he'd get clobbered. The MPs (Military Police) and SPs (Shore Patrol) arrived (about 100 or so) and attempted to board each ship and break up the madness.

They got fucking bombed.

It was great!

They became the main targets of about 3,000 guys on the "Pride of the United States Navy," the troop transport USS *Bear*, and the 2,500 or so personnel on the Naval Ship Helicopter Aircraft Carrier USS *Iwo Jima*. It was a battle that should be recorded in the annals of naval warfare. It lasted about two hours and only stopped when both sides ran out of food. It is still hard to believe the mess created and the food wasted.

But shit, was it fun!

For the record, the spirited team from the USS *Iwo Jima* won.

We continued to lay low until well after we left Okinawa and sent out one scout to see what was going on—we knew there was going to be some repercussions from the Okinawa Food War. The scout came back and said that the PT and work details had been doubled. We laid low until the coast was clear and then resumed our sea cruise.

As a side note, we learned later that the guys on the USS *Bear* slept in shifts and were sick the entire time. Apparently, the ship rolled so badly that everyone on board was seasick, and the smell was so bad that it made the rest of the guys sick too. The guys who weren't sick had to clean up after the guys who were. Morale was nonexistent and there were fights all the time. There were stampedes trying to get topside for fresh air, and the freshwater system on the boat could not keep up with the demand. Showers were allowed every four days. Word was that the food was bad and minor rationing was in effect. These guys went through about 24 days of hell after serving in Vietnam for 13 months or more.

Didn't seem fair.

Because my buddies and I were "lying low" and trying to hide out, we spent almost all of our time in the refueling room. The books, magazines, and card games passed the time, but there was a lot of time spent doing nothing. Because of this I had a lot of time to think about the last several years of my life and try to figure out what I was going to do when I got out of the Marine Corps and had to find a job. In particular, I wanted to make some sort of sense about why I'd been such an asshole when I was younger. I'd been such a rebellious and arrogant teenager that even I had a hard time believing it. I had been so incredibly angry at life. I'd put my mother through hell and it wasn't her fault. I was sorry for a lot of shit I'd caused and the hurt feelings I'd created.

I realized that losing my dad so early in life made it tough for me to be happy—no kid could be happy in that situation. The fact that I could not control my anger and instead used it in an even more negative manner is probably explained in some psychiatry book.

Well, there was no psychiatrist there at the time, and I'm not sure I would have gone to one even if there had been.

I didn't have an answer then and I still don't. I only know that I was mad, I hurt, and I lashed out. And now I was sorry. Coming home from Vietnam, I didn't feel that hurt anymore and I was no longer mad at anybody. That seemed like progress. Now I wanted to succeed in life and achieve something. I wanted to make something of myself and not just pick up where I had left off before joining the Marines. Maybe I had survived Vietnam for a reason. Now I needed to find out what that reason was.

24

Sometimes Your Heart Hurts

As we continued cruising toward San Diego, I tried to figure out how not to be the person I had been before I'd left for Vietnam. My first task was to apologize to my mother. I now felt confident that I could take care of myself and be okay in life. I'd learned to take responsibility, and I'd certainly learned discipline. I could take and follow orders. My former lack of confidence had been replaced by a sense of accomplishment. I could apply for a job and know that whoever hired me would get someone who was dedicated, willing to work, and would do what he was told. I actually felt I could be an asset instead of a liability.

But only time would tell.

About two or three days out of San Diego, the ship's PA announced that everybody who had come on board in Danang needed documentation to get off the ship. Since nobody on the ship knew we existed, we could have been in trouble. The day before we were supposed to dock in San Diego, we mixed in with guys waiting in long lines to get the paperwork necessary to get off the boat. When I got to the table where a Navy lieutenant sat, he asked my name and service number. I told him, and he looked through the mound of paperwork on the table and couldn't find any record of me. He asked if I had been processed in Danang and what my assigned number was. I answered that I had been processed but had never received my number, even after repeatedly asking. The lieutenant assigned me one and that was that.

Simple. The boat docked at Naval Base San Diego to a band and lots of people on the dock. This had been arranged by the military to welcome the troops and it was a great sight.

At last, we were home.

The pleasure, however, was short-lived.

We got off the boat, were herded onto a bunch of cattle cars, and sent to Camp Pendleton, where we were officially processed back into the world. We turned in our weapons, were searched for contraband, and were given back all the stuff we'd put into storage before we left for Vietnam. I got my uniforms cleaned, went to the PX and got all the ribbons for my uniform, and generally got myself ready to finally go home.

The USS *Iwo Jima* nearing dock in San Diego, arriving from Danang, October 1969 (Tim Fortner Collection, Vietnam Center and Archive, Texas Tech University).

The base at Camp Pendleton went out of its way to make us feel welcome. They kept the PX open 24 hours and returned our dry-cleaning in five hours. They had counselors ready to help us with travel plans and arranged a special discount for transportation to either San Diego or LA. The base had paymasters available to catch us up on our pay and had orders ready for our next duty assignments. All in all, these people and the base were wonderful. I was very grateful.

I split a cab from Camp Pendleton to LAX. At the airport, Pacific Southwest Airlines had a deal for servicemen traveling with orders for a flight to SFO for about $10. Thanks, PSA. Then I called my mom to pick me up at San Francisco and got on the jet.

24. Sometimes Your Heart Hurts

My outlook on the world and the way I felt about people changed that day.

Changed forever.

If the first part of my journey home was wonderful, the next phase was anything but.

Unfortunately, once I was back in the USA, I realized what it meant to have been in the "war nobody wanted," the "forgotten war," the "war that didn't count," the "unpopular war," among other descriptors.

President Nixon was doing his "Vietnamization" thing and pulling out of Southeast Asia. Chaos was setting in across South Vietnam, and U.S. attempts to train the South Vietnamese to fight for themselves had been a dismal failure.

The United States had entered into a war for political reasons and without a clear plan to win.

We didn't win. Not even close.

I don't think there is any question today that the Vietnam War was a really bad deal, but to fully understand that, you had to experience it in person. Today, when our military personnel come home from Iraq or Afghanistan (or any conflict), they're treated with respect and praised for their service, as they should be. Those who made the ultimate sacrifice are honored; also as it should be. There are parades and parties for today's veterans. Recognizing our fighting men and women and acknowledging them for their service is a great way to honor them. God bless our fighting men and women and thank you for your service to our country!

But in 1969, things were very different. There were massive war protests in San Francisco and New York and all across the United States. There were riots in Detroit and other major American cities. Anti-war protests and peace demonstrations took place everywhere, all the time. The American flag was being burned and young men were dodging the draft and going to Canada to avoid military service. Meanwhile, Jane Fonda was in Hanoi assisting the Communists in their effort against the United States, and people were okay with that.

Fuck her!

Even to this day, ask any Vietnam-era veteran about Jane Fonda or even mention her name and that veteran will launch into a tirade. In addition to being an actress, Fonda was a political activist and an outspoken critic of the war in Vietnam. Fonda traveled to Hanoi in July 1972 and was photographed on a North Vietnamese/Soviet anti-aircraft gun, a photo that has continued circulating for decades. Her comments at the time about the American POWs at the Hanoi Hilton were infamous. For years she has shown little to no remorse or guilt for her actions while the damage to the POWs and their families cannot be calculated.

People in the United States military faced discrimination because they wore a United States military uniform. We weren't the enemy. My entire generation of veterans bore the brunt of the anger of a cross-section of our country and without any justification. I honestly feel that situation has not changed and won't ever change.

When we were in Vietnam, we had been able to get American newspapers, either by subscription or because they were sent to the guys from relatives at home. So we were very aware of what was going on in the United States and were uncomfortably aware that a lot of people back home didn't like us or the war. But none of that was our fault. Here we were, a bunch of kids in a war zone, fighting because we took the oath of enlistment, doing our duty and serving our country, while back home some people were rioting and burning the flag.

I've got news for that whole damn group—we didn't necessarily want to be in Vietnam, but we went because it was our duty to go. We didn't shirk our obligations or responsibilities, we didn't run away, and we weren't cowards. The assholes who protested and rioted expressed their views in really ugly ways. They probably thought it was cool at the time. I sincerely hope that today, they are ashamed. They should be. If they're not ashamed, then they are still the same useless cowards they were in the '60s.

Fuck them.

I'm not saying that these people were wrong in their thinking—they had a right to express their opinions and beliefs. My issue is with the methods they employed to try to get their point across, the lasting harm they did to my generation of veterans, their total lack of respect for our military personnel, and their total disregard for the United States of America.

Does anyone think that the kids in the armed forces of the United States fighting in Iraq or Afghanistan wanted to be there? Of course they didn't. Were the wars in Iraq and Afghanistan unpopular? Of course they were. The kids fighting for the United States today are doing what they were trained to do and are protecting all of us. God bless them all.

What a difference 40 years makes.

When I returned to the United States from Vietnam and was processed out for leave from Camp Pendleton, I put on my uniform and got the flight from LA to San Francisco. I felt proud to wear the uniform of the United States Marine Corps, proud that I had served my country, proud to have served in Vietnam.

I am still proud today.

I was ready to be home and had 20 days leave before my next duty assignment. In 1969, there was no security in airports like there is today, and anyone could go anywhere within the airport. You didn't need a ticket to get

24. Sometimes Your Heart Hurts

to a boarding or arrival area; you didn't need any identification at all, and there were no security checkpoints.

When I got off the plane at San Francisco and walked toward the baggage claim, I was approached by a woman about 18 to 20 years old. She wore a white dress and had flowers in her hair. First she smiled at me, and then she began screaming and spitting on me. She screamed that I was a "baby killer," a "murderer," a "rapist," and a "war monger." She continued to spit on me and then began kicking me in the legs. There were several other people with her and they too began screaming at me.

Sadly, the other people in the area just stood by and watched. As I was warding off this woman's blows, an elderly lady came up and pulled the woman away from me. This lady was at least 75 years old and was the only person to intercede. The police showed up and told the screaming woman to leave the airport—that was it. They just told her to leave. The police never said a word to me.

Welcome home, Tim!

I was totally stunned. I would have appreciated a pat on the back when I got home, but I didn't get one. Neither did my fellow servicemen and women of the Vietnam era. Today, we still have not been recognized for our service. The truth is that the Vietnam-era veterans have *never* been welcomed home. And I am certain now that it is never going to happen, for me or for my fellow vets. America has moved on, even though for many Vietnam vets, "moving on" isn't even a possibility. Our anger continues, and will no doubt continue for the rest of our lives.

* * *

My first duty posting after Vietnam was at MCAS (Marine Corps Air Station) Yuma, where I would complete my final nine or 10 months of service. I was assigned to a maintenance squadron and worked there for about four months on both fixed wing and helicopter aircraft. The work was okay, but not particularly challenging. When a request for qualified swimmers to work as lifeguards at the enlisted and officers' pools was posted, I applied and was transferred to the Special Services Division of the Air Station. Special Services handled all extracurricular activities on base, and also controlled both the enlisted and officers' pools. The pools were open most of the year—this was Yuma, Arizona, and it got *hot*.

I was a pretty good swimmer, having taken lessons as a kid. The local chapter of the American Red Cross trained me and two others as Water Safety Instructors and then trained and qualified us as lifeguards.

In May 1970 I was assigned as NCOIC of the Enlisted Swimming Pool, MCAS Yuma. I was responsible for all areas of operation of the pool except maintenance. Each summer, the enlisted pool offered swimming lessons for military personnel, their dependents, and children. That summer my two assistant lifeguards and I taught 457 people, mostly kids, to swim.

In one of my swimming classes of 12- to 14-year-olds was a young man named Manuel Villareal. Manuel was a tall, good-looking, gangly kid and appeared very shy. He was of Mexican descent (his dad was Mexican American and his mom was from Mexico). He was at the stage where he was a little uncoordinated because of a growth spurt.

Teaching swimming to a kid who could not swim was a challenge, but teaching a kid to swim who was afraid of the water was way past difficult and required enormous patience. We started by having them sit on the edge of the pool and put their feet in the water. This wasn't as easy as it sounds. If we got past that stage, we tried to get the kids to stand in the shallow end or on the steps.

Normally, we could gain their confidence and help them overcome their fear. Once we got to that point, we could begin the actual swimming instruction. This was a delicate process and had to be handled with a lot of care and concern.

Manuel couldn't swim and was terrified of the water. His mother was a very nice woman and enrolled him in the lessons. She'd tried to get him to swim but he wasn't having anything to do with it.

I always gave a ground school at the start of each class and explained what we were going to do and asked for a show of hands from the swimmers and non-swimmers. I was then able to divide up the class accordingly.

Manuel and several other kids were in a non-swimmers group. This group required a different approach because we needed to get the kids into the water before we could teach them to swim. Some of these kids would not get within 10 feet of the water no matter what we did. We would try buckets of water at the 10-foot line and have the kids splash the water out of the bucket onto each other. We would use hoses and have the kids spray each other. Most of the time we could gain their confidence and get them to put their feet in the pool. If we could get them to that point, we had a pretty good chance of teaching them to swim.

Manuel wanted nothing to do with swimming or water—no way. He was not just scared but terrified. More than that, he was very inhibited. He always looked down and would never make eye contact. He spoke in single syllables—mainly "yes" and "no."

I tried a lot of stuff with him but couldn't gain his confidence. He would not go anywhere near the pool. The other kids began to adjust and get into the water but Manuel stayed on the concrete. The other kids made fun of him and this didn't help.

His mom was a really great lady who obviously loved Manuel. I asked her if I could keep Manuel after class and work with him and also asked her to stay too. She agreed, and on the first day, I just talked with him to try to find a way to solve his dilemma. I couldn't figure out why he was having such difficulty. I told him that swimming could be fun and that I could teach him to swim and stay safe.

Nothing doing. He wouldn't budge.

I told him that his mother wanted him to learn to swim and he was going to learn how to swim.

Nope. No way.

I gave him a private ground school and taught him to do swimming strokes on the concrete. I told him he was capable of doing this and he would be in the water in a day or two.

He was having none of it.

The next day he was with the regular class when I took him to the edge of the pool and told him to put his feet in the water. I pulled him down toward the pool and he started to cry and fight and scream. The other kids laughed at him and that made things worse. That was a really dumb-ass thing for me to do, but I was getting frustrated. But that was no excuse. It wasn't his fault he was afraid.

I had him and his mom stay after class again and continued trying. I kept telling him he could do it; he just needed to apply himself. I didn't realize at the time that I was being pretty hard on him. I was not looking at the whole situation and was really pissed off at myself for the way I was handling it. In other words, I felt like a real shit. Here I was, a guy who had been a terrible student in high school, not caring about anything, a general fuck-up, and now I was trying to teach something to a kid. So I tried to remember everything that *didn't* work with me.

This made me really think deeply and take a hard look at Manuel's situation. Here was a 12-year-old kid, and he did not want to do this. He was afraid. There was no reason to push him or force him to do something he didn't want to do.

So I changed my approach. I told him I was sorry this was so hard but that it was okay. I also apologized for pushing him so hard. If he learned to swim later, great. If not, that was okay, too. I told him not to worry about the other kids giving him a rough time. When he was ready to take the next step, I would give him a hand.

The summer classes ended and most of the kids went back to school. The pool was still open and the kids would come after school and stay until they had to go home. One day Manuel's mom came to the pool to talk to me. She told me that just before Manuel started swimming lessons, his dad had been declared missing in action in Vietnam. She said he'd withdrawn, become reclusive, and was sad and depressed. He was getting into some trouble at home and school. Since returning to school, his schoolwork was very bad and she was very worried. She hoped that getting him involved with other kids and with swimming lessons might help.

So here you have a 12-year-old whose father is missing in action, who is sad and withdrawn, does not want to "conform," and is doing poorly in school.

Hmmm.

Been there, done that.

Okay, Tim. Use your head. Help this kid if you can.

What Manuel needed was some encouragement, and to know he wasn't alone. His mother asked if I'd be willing to work with Manuel again on a one-on-one basis. I told her I'd be glad to.

The following week Manuel's mom brought him to the enlisted pool after school and we started from square one. I asked him if he'd heard any more about his father and he said no, but he knew his dad was alive and would be coming home. I asked if he hurt inside because his dad was missing. The floodgates opened and he started to cry. His mom started to cry. I started to cry. I held him until the tears stopped.

Poor kid.

I asked if he was pissed off and angry and he said yes. I asked if he was scared. Yes. I asked if there was anything he wanted to do or if he just wanted to be left alone and he said he didn't know.

I told him that if he wanted to get rid of his fear of the water and learn to swim to tell me what he thought would work and I would give it a go. I told him swimming would be something different and fun and maybe help him get his mind on something else, even if only briefly.

He told me he was afraid he'd sink (a pretty common fear, in fact) and that he was afraid the other kids would make fun of him. We decided to have his mom bring him to the pool at night after closing. The facility had lights and the pool had underwater lights. I also thought I might have a way to get him into the water while addressing his fear of sinking.

A friend of mine in Yuma had a great ski boat and we would waterski at one of the local lakes as often as possible. I had my own skis and ski vest. I asked Manuel if they had a bathtub at his house and he said he did. I gave him the ski vest and told him that even though it was a little too big for him, he could wrap it around him and get into the bathtub. I told him he could float a little bit and asked him to try it. If he could stay buoyant in the tub, the same would happen in the pool.

He came back the next day and told me he tried the vest and it was really good—he could float in the tub. I told him that when we started the lessons again, he could wear the vest and see how he felt. If he could float and wasn't scared, we'd proceed. And if he was not comfortable, we'd try something else. I told him, again, that it was okay if he didn't get into the water. We could go on a picnic instead.

24. Sometimes Your Heart Hurts

We started slowly and I got his mother involved in the lessons too. Manuel got into the water and felt okay with the vest on. But he didn't let go of the edge of the pool for a while.

Totally understandable.

I basically taught Manuel and his mom to swim together and, after a lot of false starts, Manuel overcame his fear of water, took off the ski vest, and learned to swim efficiently. He and his mom worked pretty well together and had a little fun.

He loosened up and even laughed a little. He started to make eye contact and talk a little more—not much, but an improvement over single syllables. He never became an Olympic swimmer and he never swam the English Channel.

He didn't need to.

He did finally swim across the pool, to the applause and cheers of both his mom and me. Then he smiled and swam back. He overcame his fear and realized there were people out there who would spend time with him, listen to him, and then help him make a decision. He learned that if he asked for help, somebody would respond.

I never found out what became of Manuel's missing father. I pray that it worked out but I kind of doubt that it did.

These were the hidden casualties of the Vietnam War, the casualties no one ever hears about. There were so many of them, and I have no doubt that many of those wounded souls are still hurting today, almost 50 years later.

25

Rest in Peace, Rusty

When I started looking for full-time employment after returning from Vietnam, the pickings were pretty slim. I thought that employers would be happy to have a military veteran working for them, but I put in numerous applications and got zero responses. That was quite discouraging, but I kept looking.

While I had been on leave prior to my discharge, the asshole doctor had a party at his Snob Hill house and a lot Santa Cruz's big-hitters and businessmen were there. I was at the house and walked in to say hello and heard a lot of "Atta boy!" "Great to see you, when you get out, come see me about a job!" "We got a place for you at Markley Industries when you get out!"

But then when I was finally back home and went to take them up on those offers—well, let's just say those guys had selective amnesia and suddenly there were no job openings.

Rusty, February 19, 1969, Chu Lai, Vietnam (Tim Fortner Collection, Vietnam Center and Archive, Texas Tech University).

25. Rest in Peace, Rusty

That was totally discouraging.

Through a friend of a friend, I was introduced to Lowell, a building contractor who hired me to clean up his job sites. It wasn't much of a job, but at least I could earn a little money while searching for something better. But I was still living at my mother and her asshole husband's house on Snob Hill and that did not sit well with me at all. Here I was at 22 years old, a United States Marine Corps veteran, and I was living at home working for minimum wage.

About two weeks into my work for Lowell, he told me there was an old septic tank on one of his construction sites that needed to be removed and he needed a trench dug around the whole tank. The trench was necessary to get a backhoe close enough to wrap a chain around the top of the tank, lift off the lid, drain the septic tank, and then break it up and remove the tank.

This supposed two-day job took four days, and by the fourth day, the dirt from the trench began to get wet, heavy, and really stinky. The deeper I dug, the worse the wet and smell got. The term "knee-deep in shit" has had real and intimate meaning to me ever since. I was wearing tennis shoes and jeans and the shit was past my ankles and up to my calves. My clothes were ruined and I stunk really, really badly.

At the end of the day, my hands were bleeding pretty good, my clothes smelled like shit, my shoes sloshed with the stuff, and I was exhausted. At least the job was finished. But now I had to get home. I looked over at my beautiful, red 1970 Mach I Mustang that I had purchased in Vietnam and just about cried.

I pulled off my shoes and threw them in the trench. Same with the jeans, t-shirt, socks, and underwear.

So there I was, standing naked, outside, on the job site, being watched by a few of the remaining construction people and pondering my next move. I had a canvas coat in the trunk and put it on the front seat. I used water from a hose to wash my hands, got in the Mustang, and drove eight miles home.

Naked.

I got out of the Mustang on the street in front of my house, still naked, walked to the back door and yelled for my mom. When she got to where I was, she stopped, backed up about 10 feet, stared at me, and made a face. Then she plugged her nose. Couldn't blame her. There I was, 22 years old, a United States Marine Corps veteran, and standing outside, naked, smelling like shit, in front of my mother.

Jesus!

I asked her to get the garden hose and some soap and spray me down while I tried to scrub the shit and smell off my body. When that was done, she tossed me a towel and I took a shower that lasted an hour plus, then dried off with a fresh towel. Afterward, she threw both the towels away.

At dinner that night, my mother's asshole doctor husband made the sage comment "Tim, sometimes in life you get a hard job and you just have to get through it. It will make you a better man. And it doesn't sound to me like the job was all that bad."

I slowly put down my fork, looked him in the eye, and asked, "I know you're a real famous doctor and everything, and you've done a lot of real hard jobs in your life, but have you ever dug out a septic tank full of shit and felt better for it? I'm really curious because I have been standing in wet shit for four days and I do not feel better for it."

He looked shocked and said, "Tim, you shouldn't talk that way at the dinner table!"

Because he did not like the word "shit" spoken at his dinner table, I replied, "Well then, how about 'Fuck you'? Is that better, you fucking asshole?"

That was the end of the dinner conversation and most certainly the end of my living arrangements on Snob Hill. Fortunately for me, my former high school quarterback was in Santa Cruz for a few days and I went to see him. Jerry Connors threw me three touchdown passes one year and we had remained friends. After a few drinks, he told me that there was an opening with Ocean Tennis Courts in Santa Monica and I could come work there if I wanted to.

No need to ask twice—where do I sign?

Two days later, I threw what few possessions I had in the Mustang and headed south to Santa Monica. Thinking back to my mother's asshole doctor husband, at the time I wanted to smash him in his fucking face. He was such an arrogant jerk. But now I am glad I didn't—that would have only created a big hassle for me. Two years later, he died from the rapid onset of Hodgkin's disease and the associated complications. I did not attend his funeral, did not shed a tear, and never missed him a bit.

Once I got to Santa Monica, I split a cheap apartment with another employee of Ocean Tennis Courts and learned how to build tennis courts. That turned out to be a great job with a great salary. In two years at Ocean Tennis Courts, I worked my way up to second in command and was making enough money to rent a three-bedroom condo in Marina del Rey overlooking the ocean. In late October I traded the Mustang for a brand-new 1973 Dodge Charger SE 440 that was loaded. I had "power of the pen" at most of the top nightspots in Marina del Rey including The Basement and The Second Story—the two best chick restaurants/bars in Southern California.

Ocean Tennis Courts built courts all over the United States and around the world. We did every major hotel tennis court on the Las Vegas Strip, and all of the major tennis clubs and resorts in Palm Springs. Ocean Tennis Courts built about 300 tennis courts a year and surfaced or resurfaced another 300.

The job was absolutely wild! I was promoted to company manager, got a

25. Rest in Peace, Rusty

raise to $125,000 a year, was given a commission of three percent of each job, and all of my living expenses were paid. My social life was way past great and I was living a life most people could only dream of. I was 23 years old, sitting on top of the world, and literally had life by the tail.

During that time, I got back to Santa Cruz a few times to visit friends. One night I was at one of my old haunts when I ran into a former girlfriend from high school. Her parents owned the bar/restaurant I was at and we all knew each other pretty well. Monica had been married and divorced, had a three-year-old son, and lived in the mountains just outside of Santa Cruz. She was working with her parents at the restaurant and when closing time came, one thing led to another and I spent the night with her.

Monica and I became pretty steady and I would either drive or fly back to Santa Cruz whenever possible. After five months, we started talking about a future and took the preliminary steps toward building a life together. For the first time in my life, I felt that I was going in the right direction, doing the right things, and was going to be happy with the woman I loved.

For me, this represented a major step. I was a bachelor who played around a bunch, had plenty of money, a nice car, a fantastic condo, and almost anything I wanted. But I was willing to give that up to finally settle down.

Our talks grew a little more concrete and it was pretty evident that we were going to make a big decision pretty soon. The week before Christmas, 1972, one of the tennis court jobs got rained out and, unannounced, I flew to San Jose, rented a car, and drove to Monica's house in Santa Cruz. I was going to surprise her, and I sure did.

Boy, did I ever!

When I got there, it was pretty late and the lights were out. There was a car in Monica's driveway I did not recognize. Nice car—a new yellow Pantera. I went to the front door, used my key, and went in.

What I saw was a wine bottle and two glasses on the floor and Monica sitting astride a guy on the floor, bouncing up and down, in front of the fireplace. She looked at me in shock, I looked at her in shock, the guy impaling her looked from Monica to me, and then Monica jumped up and ran to her bedroom and slammed the door. The guy on the floor grabbed his clothes, headed for the door, and split.

Well, so much for true love and a life together.

Monica came out and told me she was in love with "what's his name," that "what's his name" had a small airplane and would fly her to lunch around the state, that "what's his name," had a nice car (it was a nice car), that "what's his name" wanted to marry her and that she and I were through. Then she told me to leave.

I do not think Monica ever realized that she was about five seconds from getting killed before I turned and left her house. I could actually see myself beating the shit out of her. It was that close.

That ended that chapter. Or so it seemed. Stunned, hurt, and shocked do not begin to describe my feelings. I returned to San Jose, got a motel room, and flew back to Southern Cal the next morning.

That Christmas sucked! I flew to Hawaii for Christmas and spent most of the time at the bar at the Outrigger Hotel on Waikiki Beach. It has always been one of my favorite bars and the Mai Tais are the best. I drank a lot of them on that jaunt!

By January, I had written off Monica and had pretty much decided that girls were good for playing with but not good for staying with and I threw myself back into my work at Ocean Tennis Courts.

A couple splitting up is a pretty common occurrence, but this was the first time I had gotten so serious about someone. This prompted an introspective look at my life and I figured that, all in all, I was going to be okay. I had managed to get through high school, through the USMC and a war, had the best job imaginable, and really did not need anybody else. I was hurt but thought that would ease after a while. I just needed to get through this phase and get on with my life.

Unfortunately, "life" had something else in mind for me.

It's still just incredible to me that one day my life was as good as it could be and the next day … the crash began. And what a crash it was. I did not realize it at the time but my wild, chaotic youth, my experiences in Vietnam, and a failed relationship were going to catch up with me and send me into a spiral that would ultimately not only threaten my sanity, but also my very life.

* * *

One of the most difficult elements of my post–Vietnam life was having to watch the downward spiral of my best friend, Rusty, who had been with me through high school, the Marine Corps, and beyond. Rusty got a few odd jobs in Santa Cruz after his discharge, but small-time stuff and nothing permanent. I was able to get him hired by Ocean Tennis Courts in 1974. Working together, I began to notice that he was a little bit lethargic and slow to react in general. Pot in the '70s was used pretty heavily and Rusty used it to excess. No condemnation here—just a fact.

As time went on, Rusty became more lethargic and seemed to have lost that "good old Rusty flare." His Ford van was always dirty and mechanically marginal, but Rusty never did anything about it. His dress and appearance weren't great, either. He did laundry when he had run through all the dirty stuff and showered less than normal. None of this was terrible, but it was most certainly a change.

One evening, I found Rusty at my condo in Marina del Rey, lying on

25. Rest in Peace, Rusty

the front porch. I was able to drag him inside and lay him on the living room floor. He was breathing okay but not conscious. He was flushed and his face and arms were pretty warm. I washed his face with cold washcloths and stripped off his shirt to cool him down. After about 10 minutes, I was headed for the phone to call an ambulance when Rusty rolled on his side and vomited on the living room floor.

He started to come around and finally sat up and looked at me. He said, "Where am I?" I told him and he shook his head. He then said, "Why am I at your place?" I told him I had no clue—I found him on the porch.

He said, "Aw, shit." Then he started to shake horribly and I called an ambulance. They carted him to the hospital where he was admitted and stayed the night.

His admitting doctor asked me how long Rusty had been using heroin. I answered I had no clue. Pot, yes. Smack, no.

Rusty had either overdosed on heroin or got a bad batch. Either way, he came close to going to the other side that night. I checked him out of the hospital and he stayed at my place for a few days to recover. I had to work, so Rusty stayed there while I was gone.

On the third day, I came home to find Rusty in the lounge chair, seemingly asleep. On the table was a disposable lighter, a spoon, a glass of water, a small plastic bag with what I assumed was heroin, and a syringe.

Damn it!

Once Rusty came around, I told him it was time to knock off that crap and we would find a way to get him some help. He said he was okay and I slapped his face as hard as I could. In his earlier days, Rusty would have beat the crap out of me, but not now.

The next morning, he and I had breakfast and I took him back to the hospital to get some advice. We were directed to a drug counselor's office and she talked with us for about an hour, explaining Rusty's options and his probable further decline.

Much to his credit, Rusty enrolled in a drug program like AA that included meetings, classes, counselors, and the like. Rusty stayed the course, returned to work, and did pretty well. He still smoked pot, but everybody else seemed to be smoking it too.

Before I left Ocean Tennis Courts, Rusty decided he wanted to go a different direction, so he applied for, and got, a job with the California Department of Forestry as a firefighter. He later applied to the California Department of Corrections and was hired as a prison guard at the Sierra Conservation Center in Jamestown, California, where he worked from the late '80s to the early '90s. Unfortunately, he and I lost touch as I began my own downward spiral.

One day, years later, I got a call from Rusty's mother letting me know he had contracted Hepatitis C and was being admitted to the University of

California San Francisco Medical Center for a liver transplant the next day. He had been on a waiting list for quite a while.

It didn't take me long to figure out where he got that. More drug use. Dirty needles.

Rusty had the transplant and the operation went well. He called his mom and let her know that he was being discharged and asked that she come get him.

When she got to UCSF to pick him up, she was told that Rusty had died that morning from "post-operative complications."

Rusty was gone. It was February 20, 1997. He was 49 years old.

Rusty had led a difficult and vagabond life after being discharged from the USMC. The drug use got bad, then under control (so I thought) and then, obviously bad again.

During his time as head of the crash crew in Chu Lai, Rusty saw and experienced a lot of bad stuff that happens when planes crash, including a few close calls with burning aircraft and rescues. I know his alcohol consumption was pretty high (as was mine). I know he didn't sleep well, and smoking pot seemed to help that a little.

When I add it all up, my lifelong best friend never got the help he needed (and was entitled to), largely because he never sought help. Rusty most certainly did have thoughts and dreams from his Vietnam service that haunted him, and that led him to drugs and alcohol. His death could have been prevented. I kick myself for not knowing what was happening to Rusty and for losing touch with him.

I may have been able to help him. I think about that often.

We had a strong bond—the kind books are written about. We grew together as Marines and as men. We experienced some great times and lived life to the max.

So long, Rusty.

Damn it!

26

The Road of No Return

I was still trying to find my place in the post–Vietnam world when I drove up to Santa Cruz in March 1973 to see some friends. Unfortunately, during the trip I ran into my ex, Monica, at a local bar. She cornered me and told me that she and "what's his name" had split up and that she still loved me and blah, blah, blah…. I had only two words for her: "Fuck off." I told her to leave me alone, that she had ruined everything, and to get lost. She became hysterical and I left the bar before the situation escalated. I still had the Charger, and the burnout from the bar was pretty impressive.

My mother was out of town so I went up to her house and had a shot of Jack Daniel's. And another. And another.

And in that alcohol-induced fog, I just flat-out snapped. Really snapped. Another Jack Daniel's did little to help, and my downward spiral continued. Most of my memories of that night are vague, but at some point, I remember thinking, "Fuck it! I am tired, drunk, and depressed. I have no roots, no one I am close to, and right now I fucking hate life!"

Then I set out down the road of no return.

My mother, due to her connections from her asshole doctor husband, had a lot of Santa Cruz doctors at her disposal and had any drug or medication she wanted (wanted, not necessarily needed). A lot of recreational drugs were widely used and abused at that time. My mother had new prescriptions for Nembutal (Pentobarbital; 30 pills), Sinequan (Doxepin; 30 pills) and Seconal (Secobarbital; 30 pills).

I took the pills from her bathroom, got a full glass of Jack Daniel's on the rocks, and downed all the pills and all the Jack. It took me about 20 seconds. Ninety pills are a lot to swallow, even with the help of Jack Daniel's.

Then I had another Jack Daniel's.

This was no suicidal "gesture" on my part, no half-assed attempt to go over to the dark side—it was as serious as possible. I just felt that it was my time. Surprisingly, after I had taken the pills and booze, I felt completely okay with what I had just done. I was not scared or panicky and I had no desire to run to the bathroom and shove my finger down my throat.

Instead, I felt completely at peace. Moreover, and this will likely make all the psychiatrists out there shudder, but even to this day, I feel that the decision I made that day was the right one. I was okay with it then and I am okay with it now.

After I took the pills and booze, I left my mother's house on Snob Hill, got into the Charger, started driving, turned on the radio, and was listening to the San Francisco Giants play the LA Dodgers. It sounded like a pretty good game.

While I did not have a clue where I was going, I ended up at Woodlawn Cemetery, where my father was buried. The game was still on the radio and I parked the car near my father's grave. Today, this all seems macabre, but at the time it felt natural and right.

I turned off the motor and listened to the game for a while. The last thing I remember was that the Giants and Dodgers were tied three to three in the bottom of the ninth, Leon Wagner was batting, and the bases were loaded. There were two outs and Wagner had two strikes on him.

Tim working on a Cosworth fuel injection on a Chevron FIA sports car. September 2019 (photograph by Dennis Gray).

I got out of the car and lay down on top of my father's grave. And for what seemed like the first time in my life, I felt a warm, gentle sense of peace wash over me.

That day and night are firmly embedded in my brain, where they will stay forever. I have always felt that if a person decides that he or she wants to commit suicide, that should be their choice. But this belief is not held by most people, I realize.

(Come on, Sigmund—feel free to jump in here anytime!)

26. The Road of No Return

After lying down on my father's grave, the next thing I remember is opening my eyes and looking up at a bunch of doctors and nurses in white. I guessed I was in a hospital, but my mind was very groggy. There was some sort of mask over my face and my vision was way past blurry. People were talking loudly, asking me stupid questions. Noise was coming from every direction and the light in the room was far too bright. Some dippy nurse pinched my cheek and slapped the back of my hand. A male voice asked me what my name was. Somebody shoved a needle or something painful in my right arm. I was strapped down to a bed but felt like I was floating in the air. There was a general frantic theater going on around me.

Then I passed out.

When I regained consciousness, two nurses were at my bedside. There was still more noise and a lot of annoying beeping sounds coming from somewhere. One nurse was taking notes on a clipboard and the other was trying to change the sheets with me still in the bed.

Neither nurse would look at me. So I said, "What are you girls doing after the show?" The clipboard nurse dropped the clipboard while the sheet nurse shrieked and jumped back.

All in all, it seemed pretty funny.

The next 15 minutes were a blur of doctors, tubes, shouting, a cart rolling down a hall, being moved to another bed in a different room (I think), and ... uh, passing out again.

When I next woke up, there was a doctor standing over me asking me my name (I told him), asking if I knew what had happened (I said I thought I did), asking if I knew where I was (I did not), asking me how I felt (I didn't feel much at all). After I fully regained consciousness, he told me I was at Dominican Hospital, under a mandatory State of California 72-hour psychiatric hold.

I passed out yet again and this time when I awoke, I was in a bed in a room alone with only a few things stuck into me. I was breathing on my own and had a fucking headache the size of Seattle.

A doctor came in and introduced himself as Dr. Fitzgerald, head of psychiatry. I replied that it was great to meet him and I needed a cigarette. In those days, cigarettes were not the taboo items they are today. People could, and did, smoke anywhere. Almost everybody smoked, including Dr. Fitzgerald.

Dr. Fitzgerald gave me a cigarette, lit it for me, and began his shrink dialogue. That went on for a while and when I had heard enough, I asked when I could leave. He said that if I was a good boy and did not get violent with the staff or the other patients and showed progress, then I could leave in three days. But only if my mother would take responsibility for me.

Swell.

Dr. Fitzgerald then said, "Tim, you are something of a celebrity around here because nobody who ever took as much of that stuff as you did has lived to tell about it, and the staff is pretty impressed you got away with it! But please don't do that again."

Well, I guess there was a message there someplace. I did take a lot of pills.

The pills should have worked but didn't. The doctors were pretty puzzled about that. Guess there must be a message there, too.

I asked Dr. Fitzgerald how long I had been in the hospital and he said, "Counting this morning, five days, most of it spent in a light coma."

Holy shit! Five days? Those days are lost in my memory forever. Guess the drugs were pretty good.

The rest of the story came out from Dr. Fitzgerald and Dr. Delanne, the admitting doctor, in the next few days and went something like this.

I was found at about 2 on Saturday morning and taken from the cemetery by ambulance one-half block to Dominican Hospital. I had lain down at about 10 Friday night and the result of my stomach pumping yielded very little—all of the Nembutal, Seconal, and Sinequan had been metabolized into my system by that time. My mother was informed and told the hospital about the empty pill bottles and I guess the staff went into overdrive.

Whatever the emergency room staff did, it kept me alive. That I survived was nothing short of miraculous, and the number of people who poked their heads in the door to look at the miracle patient was pretty impressive! A few doctors wanted to know why I was not dead—I took enough crap to kill a horse.

I may have been alive, but the barbiturate hangover I had was an absolute terror. The subsequent hallucinations and nausea and a bunch of other weird symptoms were terrible. Meanwhile, I underwent three days of "therapy" and talked to several shrinks who were going to help me recover and put this incident behind me and get better, or so they promised.

So there I was in the county psych ward of Dominican Hospital. The windows and doors had very thick glass embedded with wire mesh. There were no handles on the doors to the ward and they could only be opened by a security guard who sat in an enclosed booth with a button to actuate the door openers. Apart from the security guard booth was a floor-to-ceiling gate to the outside world. I never figured out from where this gate was controlled. In other words, there was no easy way to get out of this wing of the hospital.

And the people inside there were nuts, and I mean nuts. There was a lady who had run over her kids with a car—twice. There was a lady who pulled her hair out in clumps. There were people who mumbled. There were a few people who screamed out loud. There were a couple of guys who just stared at the walls. There was a 75-year-old woman named "Kitten" who pawed everybody she came into contact with. One guy, about 40 years old, always wanted

26. The Road of No Return

to talk to me and tell me about his long relationship with Thomas Edison. He was actually pretty cool to listen to.

And there I was, right in the middle with all of them. Another nice move, Tim.

Hmmm.

I considered my options and ultimately decided to be good, not cause any problems, bullshit the staff that I was "cured," and get the fuck out of that place as quickly as possible.

On the 10th day, I received my final exam from Dr. Fitzgerald and earned my release. I said my goodbyes to my fellow inmates, went out through all the security gates and locked doors, past guards, and out into the sunshine and freedom.

Except that it was raining.

Figures.

I never did find out who won that baseball game.

So here I was, a 23-year-old veteran, fresh off a suicide attempt that almost killed me, with soon-to-be no job, no girlfriend, no future, no prospects. What the hell was I going to do now?

* * *

After being released from the hospital, I returned home and three days later drove back to Santa Monica, where I said good-bye to Jerry and the boss. Both were shocked about what had happened and didn't know what to say. Then I hired a company to clean out my condo and put my stuff in storage. I also hired a coworker to drive my Charger to Santa Cruz, with instructions for my mother to sell it. I had plenty of cash in checking and savings accounts, so money wasn't a problem.

Not knowing what to do but knowing I wanted, and needed, a clean start, I called my friend Carol, who was now living in New Jersey. I told her about everything that had happened and asked if she could put me up. She said yes and invited me to come stay.

I bought a backpack at an outdoor store, filled it with some clothes and, since I'd given up my car, went to the Santa Monica Freeway and stuck out my thumb for a ride.

Somehow, 46 days later, I arrived in Rahway, New Jersey, and spent the next six months there lost in an alcoholic stupor. I was fortunate that Carol took care of me, because I was almost totally gone and could not have taken care of myself. I think that, without her help, another major crisis, possibly even another breakdown, would have been inevitable.

I was still drinking heavily. Not as much as before, but enough to be a serious problem. Carol was a godsend, going far beyond friendship. She helped me, but she didn't take any shit from me and was actually pretty cool.

As much as I appreciated Carol's help and support, I knew I couldn't stay with her in New Jersey forever. I needed another fresh start, another chance to start over. So I woke up one morning and called a friend of mine in Hawaii, a former OTC employee who had a tennis court construction company, and asked if he had any openings. He did and invited me to come on over. Carol pulled some strings and got me a United flight from Newark to SFO to Honolulu, where my friend met me.

I worked in Hawaii for one year and then returned to Santa Cruz and started Sunshine Tennis Courts. I managed to build that company into a great business and stayed with it for 10 years, by which time I felt ready to take on yet another adventure.

I had always loved cars and driving, going back to my days doing burnouts in front of the high school and paying the price with the local police and the school administration. One night, in the mid–'70s, I was watching a car race on TV and thought to myself, "This looks easy. How hard can it be to turn left? You go straight and turn left and go straight and turn left ... and sometimes you turn left and then right—I'm sure it's not that difficult!"

So I found a racing publication and bought a 1972 or '73 Rondel Formula Atlantic car from Bobby Rahal. I entered that car in an SCCA (Sports Car Club of America) driver's school and finished first in my class of open-wheel Formula Atlantic cars. I received my provisional SCCA Novice driver's license and entered my first race.

Look out, Mario, here I come! OK, so maybe it wasn't *that* easy...

I started somewhere toward the back of the field and on about the third lap, the leaders blew by me and drove away. About three laps later, they passed me again! The course was Sears Point Raceway in Sonoma, California, and was a 2.4-mile road-racing course. On about the eighth lap (out of about 20) I spun off the circuit and that was the end of my first race. Not too smooth, but I was hooked, and knew I wanted to make this a part of my future.

I entered my second race at Portland International Raceway and started about 15th out of 30 cars. I was just hanging on when it started to rain. I struggled for a few laps in the rain, the leaders passed me, and I spun and hit the wall, wrecking the car.

And that was the end of my career racing cars. Turns out it was not as easy as it looked on TV. Go figure. But I still wanted to be involved with cars on some level. I realized that my ability to work on racecars was far greater than my ability to actually *drive* racecars, so that was the path I pursued.

In the United States Marine Corps, my MOS (military occupational specialty) was a 6242, or Avionics Electronic Systems Technician. Interestingly, I found that my military education and job in aviation and working on aircraft was amazingly similar to working on racecars, particularly in the area of aerodynamics. The mechanical aspects were almost identical. The aircraft

26. The Road of No Return

flew in the air and the racecars flew on the ground—literally. So I sold my tennis court construction company and started a racecar rental company. That business lasted for many years. In fact, my cars and drivers won just about everything on the West Coast for five years.

Motor sports continued to be a major focus of my post–Vietnam life, beginning with amateur racing, followed by professional motor sports, moving on to administration and organization, and, most recently, vintage and historical racing cars.

By the early 2000s, things for me were looking pretty good. I was happy, settled, successful, doing work I loved with people who excited and energized me. To the outside world, I had life by the tail, and yet the shadow of the Vietnam War and the horrors I had witnessed and experienced there were never far from my thoughts. In fact, those long-dormant nightmares were about to rear their ugly heads and threaten my future, and my very life, once again.

27

A Ticking Time Bomb

The story of my life post–Vietnam is really a story of two vastly different lives—the life I was living externally, visible to the outside world, and the one I was living internally, a dark, despairing reality known only to me. To the outside world, I appeared happy, well-balanced, and successful, starting and growing companies, living a fast-paced lifestyle, pursuing an exciting career in cars and racing. Yet inside, I was struggling with issues including anger, insomnia, lack of close relationships, and heavy alcohol use.

At the time, I didn't want to connect these issues to my experiences in Vietnam. And while I was aware of PTSD, post-traumatic stress disorder, I never imagined it could apply to me. After all, I had served on a relatively secure base in Vietnam, away from the worst of the fighting. So many veterans had suffered much worse than I had, especially those who had lost eyes or limbs, had severe head injuries, or otherwise been disabled in ways that were obvious and visible. While I had seen and experienced some terrible things in Vietnam, I had always considered myself fortunate in light of what might have been.

I flew as a gunner for a period of time, as did others in my squadron, and was based at a reasonably secure base in Quang Tri Province. My flights (as air crew and as an aerial gunner) were usually routine to the point of being predictable. The instances when my flights encountered enemy activity were limited, and the times when enemy activity was intense were mercifully few. I was fortunate that I did not have to fly every day, but only when the schedule put me on flight status (and when my avionics shop could spare me). In other words, I didn't feel I was in constant mortal danger in Vietnam, the way so many soldiers were.

But even considering that, on balance, my experiences in Vietnam were not the worst kind possible, there was still clear evidence early on that I had some deep-seated personal issues I was not addressing, issues that could have been related to my time in service. Some of these issues included the following:

Personal intimacy was and is an ongoing struggle. I never married or

27. A Ticking Time Bomb

had children, which is quite telling. I would have liked to have had a family, but I also felt conflicted because I did not want to be involved with anyone on a personal level, and I especially did not want the responsibility that would come along with a wife and children. I didn't want anyone relying on me or needing me in that way. I didn't want to carry that burden.

I also just do not like touching or physical contact or being close (in terms of proximity) with anyone, and that has been fairly consistent throughout my life. And there were my anger issues, too, that could destroy any relationship pretty quickly as I often found it hard to control my temper.

And it wasn't just romantic relationships I struggled with; even simple friendships I found challenging. Any friendship I did manage to strike up remained guarded or cautious at best. I have always been able to maintain meaningful relationships with a few key people, and that has been enough to keep me going. But of course, I also knew I was missing out on so much by not having close friendships and more intimate relationships.

Meanwhile, I also struggled with chronic insomnia. I don't recall having it while I was in Southern California working for the tennis court company, but I started to notice it right after I sobered up a bit and went to Hawaii to work on tennis courts with my friend. I was using alcohol to knock me out and numb my feelings, but even so, that was the beginning of many sleepless nights that continued to plague me for years, growing worse over time, and that remain a menacing ailment today. I tried medication for my insomnia, but that can be tricky because of the many side effects, not to mention the highly addictive nature of the drugs. So I just struggled, adding sleeplessness to my list of very private worries and concerns.

By 2008 I was also dealing with some problems with my back and some mild hearing loss, both of which seemed related to my time in Vietnam. The partial hearing loss, I believe, was a direct result of working around helicopter turbine engines without the proper protection. When flying, I wore a flight helmet and was protected from the extreme noise and frequencies, but not when working in the shop. Near-constant exposure to loud noise had clearly taken its toll.

In terms of my back, I was in constant, almost excruciating pain. I believe this pain was a result of the time I spent in Vietnam wearing a bullet bouncer protection vest weighing approximately 30 pounds while flying as a .50-caliber door gunner and air crewman.

Imagine strapping on something of that size and weight, then having to jump three or four feet (or more) out of a hovering helicopter, run to a wounded Marine and help him back into the helicopter, and then, still wearing the bullet bouncer, carry a stretcher with the wounded Marine from the helicopter to the medical facility on a hospital ship. Then imagine doing that again and again and again. Coupled with this, imagine the numerous hard landings we endured aboard those helicopters. No wonder my spine was paying the price so many years later.

Because the hearing and back issues seemed clearly linked to my time in Vietnam, I decided to approach the VA to find out what, if any, benefits I might be eligible for. I could not have imagined at that point how that decision would change my life forever.

* * *

Tuesday, July 1, 2008, found me in Seaside, California, at the Monterey County Veterans Affairs Office, meeting with Veterans Affairs Service Officer William Zeigler, a military and veteran claims representative, to discuss filing a claim related to my back problems and hearing loss.

Mr. Zeigler was a tall, heavyset African American man with a full beard and a warm smile. His friendly demeanor quickly put me at ease. The interview began with a series of routine questions about my health status, tests and treatments I had received, and so on. We also talked about my time in Vietnam, what my tour of duty was like, what types of experiences I had had, and so on. All very friendly and routine, essentially a "get to know you" session, and I appreciated his genuine interest as he busily jotted notes while we spoke. But then, suddenly, the mood changed when Mr. Zeigler sat up straighter and cleared his throat. "Mr. Fortner, did you experience any 'stressors' while in Vietnam?" he asked carefully.

Hmm. What a strange question. "What do you mean by stressors?" I asked.

"A stressor would be any incident during which you may have had anxiety or fear due to a situation potentially harmful to yourself," Mr. Zeigler explained.

Of course I had been exposed to harmful situations—it was a war, after all. "Why do you ask?" I posed, trying not to sound defensive. "I came in to see about filing a VA disability claim for my back and my hearing loss."

He looked me squarely in the eye and replied, "Because, Mr. Fortner, after talking with you, I feel you may have a valid claim for disability due to PTSD, or post-traumatic stress disorder."

What the fuck! Is he kidding? I was furious and struggled not to lash out. "I *do not* have PTSD," I replied, measuring my words through gritted teeth. "I know several people who suffer from it, but I'm not one of them."

"Mr. Fortner, please, don't get upset," he said, then quickly glanced over his notes. "I am only asking because you answered some of my questions about your Vietnam service indicating that you were a helicopter door gunner, had several strike flights, and were awarded the Air Medal for a mission that was hostile, during which you received enemy fire. These experiences could make a case for you having PTSD," he explained.

27. A Ticking Time Bomb

I could not believe what I was hearing. "Look, Mr. Zeigler," I began, still trying not to explode, "lots of guys in my squadron went on missions that took enemy fire. Not a big deal! It happened all the time and went with the job. *I do not have PTSD.* Let's just get a disability claim filed for the other items, okay?"

"Okay, okay." He backed down. "We will fill out the paperwork and submit it to the VA." He paused, looking uncertain. "But, as a favor to yourself, I suggest you schedule an interview in Palo Alto to be evaluated for PTSD. Just to be sure. If you don't have the condition, that's great. And if you do, then you may be eligible for disability benefits from the VA."

"Fine." I was still fuming as Mr. Zeigler filled out the paperwork for my back and hearing claim. After he finished, I quickly signed the documents and left. Once outside, I took several slow, deep breaths, trying to calm down. I went to my car, got in, and just sat for a while, trying to compose myself before turning the key and starting the engine.

Why did his mentioning PTSD upset me so much? I wondered. *Could* I have PTSD? It was hard for me to even consider that possibility. I was strong, I was tough, I was a guy. PTSD was for weaklings, wasn't it? For guys who were emotionally fragile, unable to cope with the harsh reality of war.

And deep down I knew there was an element of guilt, too. I had had a relatively "easy" posting in Vietnam, especially compared to guys engaged in hand-to-hand combat, so maybe on some level I felt I didn't "deserve" PTSD; that should be reserved for guys who faced horror and death every single day and somehow survived but returned home forever changed.

My head was still spinning by the time I finally felt composed enough to drive home. I never would have believed, that sunny afternoon in 2008, that before long I would find myself saying a profound and heartfelt, "Thank you, Mr. Zeigler. You knew exactly what you were doing."

At that point, I had no idea how much longer, more difficult, and more convoluted my personal post–Vietnam journey would be, a journey that would leave me with a new perspective on myself, on PTSD, and on the reality of what I had experienced during the war in Vietnam.

* * *

On the advice of William Ziegler, in September 2008 I received notification that I was scheduled for an appointment to see Dr. Peter Berman, a clinical psychologist at the VA Palo Alto medical facility, to be evaluated for PTSD. *Just swell.* I was not looking forward to the appointment, but I *was* looking forward to finally getting some answers.

The appointment with Dr. Berman was fairly routine. He seemed like a caring person, and he asked thoughtful questions and took the time to really listen to my answers. At the end of the appointment he told me that, based on our conversation, he was convinced I had PTSD. I was surprised to hear him sound so certain, and I also admitted that I found the idea of being diagnosed with PTSD both alarming and sobering.

Sometime later I was able to secure a copy of Dr. Berman's notes from that appointment, and what I read in that report shocked me. His conclusions and observations about me included the following:

- Difficulty falling asleep
- Difficulty staying asleep
- Nightmares several times a week
- Problems with memory and concentration
- Difficulty focusing
- Some anger and irritability issues
- Depression
- Flashbacks
- Strong startle response
- Social isolation
- Alcohol abuse

Dr. Berman also noted that I was mildly anxious during the interview, with sad and depressed mood and effect. The diagnosis he submitted to the Veterans Administration, which I only became aware of later, was "Axis 1 psychiatric diagnosis of PTSD that was directly related to combat in Vietnam."

At the end of our appointment, Dr. Berman suggested that I get counseling to help manage my symptoms, but if you know me, you know I chose not to do that. Remember, I am a guy and guys don't do that stuff, or so I thought. Looking back now, I am certain I was in denial about my diagnosis, but this was denial coupled with the real fear that I might actually have a serious problem. I still viewed PTSD as a weakness, something that didn't happen to *real men* like me.

Following my appointment with Dr. Berman, I began questioning myself very deeply and uncovered horrible self-doubts. These intense feelings led me to look back and see that so much of my life post–Vietnam was filled with ordinary, emotionally neutral instances and experiences that were turned into negatives, either by myself, or worse, by my (totally unfounded) perception of other people's negative feelings toward me. It was like I had a chronic chip on my shoulder, always expecting the worst of people and situations. My attitude was uniformly terrible and I was closed off from allowing any good things into my life. Was it possible that PTSD was the root of my non-social, semi-reclusive, and self-protective approach, and my inability to be close to anyone in a relationship?

The closer I looked, the more I saw evidence that could point to PTSD. In addition to my status as never married and my issues with intimacy, I listed the following characteristics and dysfunctions that could be evidence of previous trauma:

- Heavy alcohol use
- Breakup with Monica
- "Devil may care" attitude and inability to think about or plan for the future as a young man
- Suicide attempt in 1973
- Dropping out of life and getting rid of all my possessions post-suicide attempt
- Gradual dissolution of relationship with my mother
- Limited social activities
- Walking away from a great job and hitchhiking to New Jersey
- Ongoing anger and irritability

Hmmm. Not a pretty list, is it? I could no longer deny that I had a problem. But if I did have PTSD (and that was still a big "if" in my mind, at that point), what could have triggered it? What constituted the "trauma" that led to "post-traumatic?" Here again I made a list of possible triggers:

- My father's sudden, shocking death, on my 13th birthday
- The helicopter crash I should have been on
- Flying 24 Strike Flight combat missions
- Being ambushed during one medevac under fire
- Getting shot at numerous times
- Falling out of a helicopter followed by that weird, dissociative, "out-of-body" experience
- The terror of night troop extractions
- Being in close proximity to the fragging of G/Sgt. Pleen
- The medevac missions where Marines died
- Rocket attack during troop insertion
- The immense responsibility while on guard duty at night (while being totally untrained for the task)
- Being physically and verbally attacked, spit on, and kicked at SFO Airport upon my return from Southeast Asia

Seeing all this written down really opened my eyes to how much real trauma I had either experienced directly or witnessed firsthand, beginning with my father's death, and particularly during Vietnam. It had always been difficult for me to think about, talk about, or even acknowledge these traumatic events. Again, I think this was the "guy code" at work, always needing to "man up" or "toughen up" rather than admit pain, fear, or grief.

Following my appointment with Dr. Berman and his diagnosis that my symptoms matched the criteria for PTSD, on February 9, 2009, I received notification that the Veterans Administration had granted me a 70 percent disability judgment for service-connected PTSD with secondary depression and alcohol abuse. My hearing loss and back pain claims were denied. How ironic, the two concerns that sent me to the VA in the first place—back pain and hearing loss—ended up being virtually insignificant, while the condition I barely believed existed—PTSD—was now a major component of my life.

I was fortunate to have received my answer, 40 years after Vietnam, but a big question remained: "How many of my fellow veterans are suffering from PTSD and don't know it, have not gotten help, or have simply 'checked out' of society?"

I see the reality almost daily in the town that I currently live in. I see it in their appearance, in their scraggly beards and long hair, and especially in their vacant eyes and the way they walk. That pain, quite simply, is not fixable, and stands out in every Vietnam-era veteran I have ever met. It saddens me to think about all my brothers-and-sisters-in-arms for whom the war will never truly be over.

28

Adding Insult to Injury

It was a relief to have been granted my 70 percent service-related disability for PTSD in 2009, but over the next few years I still found myself struggling with the various issues that had plagued me for years. One of my biggest problems continued to be chronic insomnia. I found it virtually impossible to get a decent night's sleep, which left me frustrated and miserable at night and exhausted and irritable during the day. I knew there were sleep medications available, but I didn't trust them, because of the potential side effects and other concerns.

Finally, in January 2011, my primary care doctor arranged for me to meet with a social worker at the VA in Palo Alto to discuss possible treatment options for my insomnia. I could never have imagined how disastrous my session with social worker Mary Bahnhof would turn out to be, or what a huge setback it would represent in my personal journey with PTSD.

To provide a bit of background, I had been told I would be meeting with a social worker. When Ms. Bahnhof came to the waiting room to get me, she told me her name but not her title. Her own office was unavailable for some reason, so she said we were going to use a different office. That office had a doctor's nameplate on the door, so I just assumed Ms. Bahnhof was a doctor, not a social worker.

During our 90-minute meeting, Ms. Bahnhof was curt and dismissive, never seeming to care about me or my problems. Regarding my insomnia, she recommended some Hindu breathing techniques and tension release exercises, which I told her I would consider, even though they were similar to other techniques I had already tried with only limited success. When I asked about my chronic joint pain, she recommended I join a health club, which I had neither the time nor the money to do.

Toward the end of the appointment, I said I had a question about PTSD. I felt compelled to ask, even though she had me feeling that I had gone over my allotted time and was keeping her from her next appointment.

"So this is a bit of a 'fishing expedition,' looking for answers and possible causes for my insomnia," I explained. "How 'post' does the post have to be in PTSD? I'm wondering if it's possible that there could be any connection between my insomnia and PTSD."

"The symptoms of PTSD can manifest as much as 20 to 30 years after the triggering event," she replied. But then she continued, with conviction, "But you do not have PTSD."

She claimed that, based on my written answers on the information sheet I filled out and from her own observations during our meeting, I did not meet the diagnostic criteria for PTSD. She said that in order for me to have PTSD, I would have had to have experienced "trauma" to account for the "T" in PTSD. She then gave several examples of trauma, such as being held hostage by a person with a shotgun at a bank, being told to kill or having killed a baby, being told to kill or having killed an old man and seeing his wife running away, having the person next to me disappear, or, finally, being shot at every day.

I sat there in shock, trying to absorb her words. What the hell was going on? I could only conclude that her comments about baby killing, killing an old man and his wife running away, the person next to me disappearing, and being shot at every day were references relating to Vietnam.

Without a doubt, I had experienced Marines dying, being shot, killed, and being blown up very close to me, within approximately 50 to 100 meters. So not sitting right beside me, but close enough. This happened on two occasions.

Based on Ms. Bahnhof's rude and dismissive comments, I could only assume she believed I hadn't experienced any real trauma and nor did I exhibit any symptoms of PTSD. I made my assumption based on her interpretation of the forms I filled out and by whatever criteria she used to ascertain the definition of trauma.

If she had bothered to ask, I would have explained that, along with my duties as an avionics technician, I served as an aerial gunner on a Marine Corps CH46-D Sea Knight helicopter, flying more than 250 separate, documented missions/sorties/flights (the real total was closer to 525).

Regarding the missions flown in Southeast Asia, a bit of explanation might be helpful. Flight missions or sorties were counted differently than they had been in World War II, where each takeoff and landing was counted as one mission, and so 20 missions (in that time period) was a lot. But in Southeast Asia, each sortie was counted as leaving one place to go to another.

This meant that if a flight/mission left from Quang Tri to Fire Base Alpha, that counted as one mission/sortie. If that same aircraft then went from Fire Base Alpha to Camp Carroll, that counted as a second mission/sortie. If that same aircraft then went from Camp Carroll to the Rockpile, that counted as three missions/sorties, and so on. This meant that one aircraft and crew could fly five to 10 missions per day.

28. Adding Insult to Injury

Many of these missions were med-evac missions, some carried out under hostile conditions and often while taking enemy fire. In addition, I flew numerous troop insertion and troop extraction missions, and two emergency troop extractions involving enemy action.

I helped load wounded and dead Marines onto my helicopter and then off-load those Marines at either C-Med/Quang Tri or the USS *Sanctuary* or the USS *Repose* hospital ships. I held temporary battle dressings on wounds so horrible and bloody that only a doctor should see them. I saw Marines wounded, dying, and dead, before my very eyes. I was awarded the Air Medal for an emergency med-evac mission flown into heavy enemy fire. I was awarded the numeral 24 to be worn on the Air Medal, signifying the number of Strike Flight missions I flew. I was awarded my Combat Aircrewman's Wings with three "Strike Flights."

And yet, after a brief conversation, Ms. Bahnhof could tell me with absolute certainty that I didn't have PTSD? I left the meeting that day feeling the same way I had when I returned home from Vietnam and was spat upon at the San Francisco Airport. How dare she! It had taken me years, decades, in fact, to even begin to accept that I might have PTSD, and here was a woman who, after knowing me for all of ninety minutes, basically decided that I was perfectly fine and, by extension, that I was receiving government benefits that I had neither earned nor deserved.

This appointment sent me into an emotional tailspin that destroyed much of the progress I had been making. I was so angry, so furious, I could barely control myself. I had gone to Ms. Bahnhof about *insomnia*, for God's sake; who was she to suddenly decree that I did not, and, moreover, could not, have PTSD?

I was still feeling disgust, anger, and dismay over my consult with Ms. Bahnhof when, a few months later, I was able to get a copy of the report and progress notes she had submitted to the VA regarding our meeting. Perhaps unsurprisingly, the document was full of mistakes, misrepresentations, and gross inaccuracies. I wasn't sure if she hadn't been listening during our conversation, or if she simply misunderstood everything I had said, or if she had some ulterior motive for writing a report that portrayed me as someone who was unmotivated and rigid, unwilling to compromise or change, even for my own benefit.

Not only was I furious about her inaccurate and unfair report, I worried what effect this report might have on my standing with the VA. Could my benefits be jeopardized by her alleged findings? I had worked too hard and endured too much to allow that to happen.

So I sat down and wrote a letter to the patient advocate representative at the VA clinic in Monterey, going point by point through Ms. Bahnhof's report, challenging and refuting what I perceived as her gross inaccuracies.

My objective was to have the document permanently removed from my VA records. I was concerned that if another healthcare professional in the VA Health Care System read the Multidisciplinary Assessment notes taken by Ms. Bahnhof, it was entirely possible that I could be perceived in a negative and inaccurate light.

Specifically, I wanted to challenge her note that "Pt. [patient] then went into a long description about being service connected for PTSD. He admitted at the end that he had a fellow comrade blow up next to him." This was blatantly untrue. There was no "long description"; in fact, I only mentioned PTSD near the end of the interview, and I did not say anything remotely close to, "had a fellow comrade blow up" next to me. This was a phrase used as an example by Ms. Bahnhof, mentioned near the end of the interview as an example of something that might cause trauma. I have never used the phrase "fellow comrade" in my life.

I also took issue with her statement that I "denied current suicidal or homicidal thoughts." Even though my records indicated my suicide attempt in 1973, she never specifically asked me about suicide during our session. So how could I deny something that never came up in our conversation?

Her diagnostic impressions were positive for insomnia and alcohol abuse but ruled out depression and anxiety—also inaccurate assessments on Ms. Bahnhof's part. Under "Recommendations and Initial Plan," she wrote, "Pt. currently does not want future appts. So no treatment plan." This statement was accurate only in that I had been under the impression, when our session began, that I was speaking with a qualified physician and not a social worker. When I realized that Ms. Bahnhof was not a doctor, I shut down and told her that I did not want to see her again. But clearly, her written comments provided a very different impression of our meeting, especially regarding my disposition when the meeting ended.

Now that I had my thoughts organized and down on paper, I was ready to take the next steps. My anger hadn't abated, but it was now being channeled into positive action. I had come too far, and achieved too much, to let one underinformed person bring me down.

* * *

I was still fuming after I wrote that letter to Mary Bahnhof, but I contemplated for a long time before sending it. I knew I was playing with dynamite, so to speak, and I was somewhat on edge as far as what the potential negative repercussions of mailing the letter could be. So I made another appointment with Dr. McMann, my therapist, and explained to her what had happened.

After reading my letter, Dr. McMann was more than distressed and, in my opinion, in disbelief about Ms. Bahnhof's actions. Dr. McMann requested that I not mail the letter and asked instead if she could personally handle the matter. Both Dr. McMann and Ms. Bahnhof worked in the same building and they knew each other.

I told her that was okay with me, and that ended that. I am positive that the issue was addressed with Ms. Bahnhof by Dr. McMann in the proper manner. Dr. McMann and I did not talk about that in future appointments—as far as I was concerned, case closed, and it was time to move on.

Sometime after that incident, Dr. McMann transferred to the Palo Alto VA Hospital. I then began seeing Dr. Adam Karwatowicz, whom I continue to see, and who was and is a great help to me.

Frankly, the whole episode with Ms. Bahnhof came very close to pushing me over the edge, mentally. Following our meeting, I began to experience crushing self-doubt, horrible feelings of guilt, and utter confusion about what to believe, WHO to believe, and what had actually happened!

I was quite lucky because my Veteran's Administration doctors were more than supportive as I worked through this ordeal. It's chilling to consider how one person's offhand and inconsiderate remarks can have a lasting and devastating effect on a vulnerable person that can last for years.

After the experience with Ms. Bahnhof, my downward spiral continued. My PTSD seemed to be getting worse, taking an increasingly destructive toll on my overall life and functioning. I reached a breaking point in 2012 when I had an incident with my then-boss that ended up having serious long-term consequences.

At the time I was working as an independent contractor at a company that restores classic and historic racing cars. My employer in this position was also my longtime friend, and our relationship involved some give-and-take on the work and organization of projects. Normally, this was a healthy and productive relationship for both of us.

The incident that changed everything started innocently enough. I was chatting with my employer/friend about a job that needed to move a little faster. I suggested that we jointly jump on the project so we could get it done quicker and have two sets of eyes on it. My employer replied that there were other projects in progress that could not wait. I rationalized to him that when we got the project in question done, we could both jump on the other projects together, rather than singularly, and therefore accomplish all of the pending jobs much sooner. He disagreed, said he was the company owner and that was how it was going to be.

So I said, "Okay, sounds good. I need help getting the gearbox off the motor." He replied he was working on something else and it would have to wait. He intimated (but did not say it outright) that if I couldn't handle the project, I should find something else to do and he would do it.

Okay, but the project I was on was going to stop, or at least get slowed down. So I let him know, one more time, that we were wasting time and that together we could accomplish a lot more than singularly. My tone was neutral and professional, and I wasn't angry, or abusive.

He let me know the conversation was over. I reacted quickly, and for an instant, I reached toward his throat with both hands but immediately pulled back. My intent was certainly to hurt him. It was a flash of total frustration, but I realized that if I continued and did hurt him, I would go to jail for assault. So instead I said, "Okay. I am giving you my two weeks' notice, effective two weeks ago." Then I got all my stuff together and walked out, angry, fuming, but fortunately still in control.

Believe it or not, my employer and I are still friends today and have a good relationship. We have even done some projects together since I left. But at that point, in 2012, I had to wonder what was wrong with me and what the hell I was doing. Here I was, walking away from yet another well-paying position with nothing planned for the future. Just like I had done so many years earlier, when I left a great job building tennis courts, sold everything I owned, and hitchhiked to New Jersey, where I fell into an alcohol-induced oblivion that lasted six months. And now here I was, more than 30 years later, doing something similarly self-destructive.

In short, I had just shot myself in the foot. Again. Why? Why had I been so rash and impulsive? I liked my job, liked my boss, liked what I was doing. Why throw it all away in a moment of ire? Was it frustration? Lack of communication? Ego? Self-sabotage? PTSD? I really didn't know. What I did know was that I felt absolutely no remorse or regret for walking away, even though I had put myself in a situation that was going to hurt me financially. I also knew for certain that I was never going to work for a "boss" again. That part of my life was over. I couldn't risk being in a situation again where I felt the compulsion to hurt someone. What if, next time, I wasn't able to stop myself? What if I couldn't will my hands to stop as they moved toward someone's throat?

It was time for a reevaluation and, if necessary, some intervention. All the signs were there that my PTSD was getting worse and that I needed more help. So with a heavy heart, I made an appointment to see Dr. Peter Berman at the VA again.

29

A Light at the End of the Tunnel

When I met with Dr. Peter Berman again in December 2012 at the Palo Alto Veterans Hospital, I told him what was going on in my life and the issues related to PTSD that were still affecting me, especially how my anger was becoming harder to control. He was sympathetic and listened thoughtfully, taking my concerns seriously.

Dr. Berman agreed that my PTSD symptoms had worsened and were seriously impacting my overall life and ability to function. He said he was going to submit his recommendation for an increase in my Veterans Administration disability benefit for combat-related PTSD. This was a sobering thought, but I knew I needed the financial support and the psychiatric help.

I was later able to get a copy of Dr. Berman's notes from that meeting. He noted that my PTSD was still present, as from before, along with secondary alcohol abuse as a means of self-medicating. My GAF (global assessment of functioning) score had gone down from 46, as tested in November 2008, to 38.

The GAF scale goes from 1 (the worst—completely nonfunctional) to 100 (a perfect score—superior functioning in all areas). According to the scale, a score of 31 to 40, where I now was, indicates: "Some impairment in reality testing or communication OR major impairment in several areas, such as work or school, family relations, judgment, thinking, or mood."

His final remarks were as follows: "Patient presents today with worsening symptoms of PTSD and more difficulty in his social and occupational functioning. PTSD symptoms include problems with poor sleep, nightmares, problems with anger and irritability, sadness and depression, difficulty in interpersonal relationships, he has never been married, flashbacks to Vietnam, self-medication with alcohol, and feelings of sadness and depression."

Damn. It wasn't a pretty picture. But it was the truth. I didn't look forward to another go-round with the VA, but I knew I had to stick with it, no matter what obstacles they threw in my way.

Over the next several months I received letters from the VA advising

Tim salmon fishing on the Smith River, November 2011.

me that my request for an increase in my disability benefit was being looked into and they would advise me when a decision had been reached. This took until 2014, when the VA notified me that my claim for an increase in disability was denied because I did not "meet the criteria" for the increase. While I wasn't surprised, I was upset and disappointed, especially since Dr. Berman had been so certain that I *did* in fact meet the criteria.

29. A Light at the End of the Tunnel

Next, I went to my veterans service representative in Monterey, who advised me to resubmit the claim, which I did. After Dr. McMann was transferred to the Palo Alto VA facility, I began seeing Dr. Adam Karwatowicz at the VA Monterey Clinic and explained to him what was happening with my claim. Given Dr. Berman's recommendation, Dr. Karwatowicz was quite surprised by the VA's decision. Dr. Karwatowicz indicated that he could push this forward by himself and, if necessary, get local congresspeople involved. I was really touched to see his level of caring and concern.

During this time, I also joined the Disabled American Veterans organization and enlisted the aid of one of their staff to push forward my claim/request for an increase in disability rating. I was a "man with a mission," determined to fight for what I had earned through my service.

The DAV paperwork was submitted and nothing happened. I was told that there was a "backlog" in the VA system and that it could be three to five years before any decision was made. Three to five years! And this backlog didn't just affect me, it affected probably tens of thousands of veterans who relied on VA disability to stay alive. They certainly couldn't afford to wait three to five years!

After several trips to Oakland and telephone calls to the DAV, I got mad at the "system" and wrote a three-page letter to then–President Obama, explaining what it was like to be a disabled Vietnam vet and how we couldn't afford to wait for help. I explained that a three-to-five-year backlog for appeals to the Veterans Administration was a joke and that I was pissed off. I sent the letter registered mail.

About two months later, I got a form letter response from the White House, and answered that letter with one of my own explaining that I did not like form letters. At the time, I thought that my appeal was destined for rejection and that no matter how much noise I made, it was not going to happen.

But my letter did get action. And for that, I thank President Obama.

I continued to see Dr. Karwatowicz and explained that the delay of three to five years was unacceptable, and if the VA had that big of a backlog, there were even bigger problems on the horizon. I emphasized that many veterans don't have five years to wait! I let him know that I had written to President Obama. Dr. Karwatowicz got in contact with the head of Veteran Services for Monterey County and set up an appointment for me.

I met with George H. Dobson, Director of the Monterey County Military & Veterans Affairs Office, and he gave me some options. One option was that I could request a hearing, on-camera, and explain my case. Option #2 was to request a face-to-face hearing. If I chose the face-to-face option, the hearing would be in Washington, D.C., and I would have to pay all of the expenses. I would be allowed access to all of the medical and psychological records at my disposal and be allowed to include any witnesses I chose. It was a lot to consider, but I had come this far, so I went for option #2, anticipating the chance to publicly plead my case.

So I took a deep breath and then took the plunge. The paperwork was submitted. At that point, I was in the hands of others. All I could do was wait. Wait, and hope.

Two weeks later, I was driving from Sonoma to Santa Cruz when I got a telephone call from Jane Sherman of the Veterans Administration Regional Claims Office in Sacramento. Ms. Sherman asked if this was a good time to ask me some questions. "As good a time as any," I replied, and she proceeded to ask me questions for about 40 minutes.

One of the questions was about my employment and if I was really going to physically harm my former employer. My answer was that I was very close to doing just that. She also asked me about marriage, relationships, and so on, and she asked if I could apply for a job and work for someone else without losing my temper. I told her that I honestly did not know, but at that point I was still self-employed and didn't plan to work for anyone else ever again. The questions were very specific and at the end she told me that she had the authorization to make a decision in my case. Did I agree to allow her to do so?

I agreed, but with the caveat that if I did not like her decision, my rights to appeal were not taken away. I was advised by her that if her decision went against me, I would still be able to pursue my claim. She advised me that her decision could take some time. "How long?" I asked.

She said, "Three weeks," and I remarked that that was a lot better than three to five years! That conversation with Ms. Sherman was quite heartfelt and I feel that she was genuinely concerned and was trying her best, not just for me, but for all veterans.

Just as she was ending the call, she asked me, "Why did you write to the White House about this matter?" My reply was that I was pretty furious about the lack of progress in any type of timely manner in my case. So I chose to go right to the top.

About five days after my conversation with Ms. Sherman, I was checking my bank account online and found a large deposit had been made to my account. That deposit was from the U.S. Treasury for retroactive compensation for my VA claim for PTSD. *What? Could it be? After all this time!*

That was how I found out that I had been granted an increase from 70 percent to 100 percent VA Service-Connected Disability for PTSD. Later that week I received official notification via a letter from the VA informing me of their decision. It was February 2015. And for this Vietnam veteran, after more than 40 years, it finally felt like coming home.

Epilogue:
Coming Full Circle

In 2015 I moved from California to Oregon, and in 2017, I moved back to California, to a small town right on the Pacific coast and close to the Oregon border. I'm still adjusting to my "new normal" as I continue treatment for service-related PTSD, and I remain active in several veterans' organizations.

To an outsider, my life today must seem nearly perfect, or if not perfect, then at least highly desirable. My home on the beach is beautiful—warm, soothing, inviting, and so luxurious that someone recently offered to buy it for $1.5 million, but I wouldn't part with my little piece of paradise for any price. I'm doing fine financially with a job that provides reasonable income, along with a $10,000 Rolex given to me as a bonus for my racing work. I own a

Tim with his brand-new 2019 Corvette.

new 2019 Ford Escape and just took delivery of a 2019 Corvette. I'm debt-free (outside of one car loan). Based on all this, one might think that I am on the top of the world and really happy.

Think again. I'm grateful for what I have, and know that I have been fortunate in many ways. And yet I still struggle with close relationships, with insomnia, with other symptoms of PTSD. I take life day by day and try to look forward to good things for the future. Sometimes that's a challenge, but I'm a fighter, and a survivor, and I don't plan to quit anytime soon.

* * *

In 2015, I finally experienced something that really brought my time in Vietnam home to me full circle. I was living in California and traveled to Texas Tech University in Lubbock so I could donate my photographs and other artifacts from my time in Vietnam to the university's Vietnam Center and Archive. I received a wonderful reception there, and everything went very smoothly. So smoothly, in fact, that I finished earlier than expected, so I decided to book an earlier flight home rather than stay over another day. I called Southwest Airlines and got a flight to San Francisco via Dallas. And here's where serendipity comes in.

Southwest doesn't assign seats; it's first come, first served. I was the first person to board the connecting flight from Dallas to San Francisco, so I took the front bulkhead seat with all the legroom so I could stretch out during the flight. Just as the last passengers were boarding, a lady asked if the seat next to me was taken. I told her it wasn't, so she sat down. I didn't think much of it and barely glanced at her.

The plane took off and the man on the aisle seat, a Caucasian guy in his 60s, struck up a conversation with the woman next to me. I happened to hear him mention that he'd gone to Hanoi 10 years ago to see what it was like. This piqued my interest, so I started to eavesdrop a little bit. Finally, I politely asked the guy why he went to Hanoi. He explained that he liked history and wanted to see Hanoi and learn more about the war. I asked if he went to the south, to Danang or Saigon, and he said no, just North Vietnam. He went on to say how the Vietnam War was a mistake, the United States should not have been there, and so on. He wasn't badmouthing or anything, just stating his opinion.

The lady asked him a few questions and I tuned them out, turning back to the book I had been reading. After about 20 minutes of them chatting about cooking and where they lived and other topics, the lady asked me why I had asked about Hanoi. I looked over, noticed that she was Asian, and asked her nationality. "Vietnamese," she replied. I told her that I had served in Vietnam.

I went back to my book, but then the lady tapped me on the arm and asked when I had been there. I told her and then asked if she had been born

27. Epilogue: Coming Full Circle

in the United States or in Vietnam. She answered, "Vietnam." I asked her how she came to the USA, and the story she told me was incredible.

The year was 1975 and she was nine years old, living with her family in a village outside Saigon. Her father was in the government in some relatively low position. He knew the North Vietnamese were close to taking Saigon and had plans to leave the country when that time came. He had packed clothing and provisions for his family, which included four children, his wife, his mother, and his grandmother. (His wife's mother was in North Vietnam.)

The woman then described how her father came home one night and said they had to leave immediately. They went to the harbor and got on a boat that had been prearranged and put out to sea. They were on that small boat for several days.

Saigon fell the night they left, April 30, 1975.

This woman and her family were picked up by a cargo ship. She and her family had to climb the square rope boarding ladder or net to get up into the ship. One child from another family fell off the net and into the sea but was rescued. Another woman, a nun, also fell into the sea and was rescued by someone on the boat.

They spent days on the ship, stopping in several countries before landing in either Okinawa or Guam (I think she said Guam). Then she and her family went through some sort of processing and ended up in the United States. Apparently, there were sponsors waiting for Vietnamese families that had gotten out. The woman later became a resident alien. She married a veteran who had served in Iraq during the first Iraq war.

I told her how very fortunate she was to have gotten out of Vietnam and she agreed. We spoke for the rest of the trip about her experiences and her family. Near the end of the flight, she asked me what I had done in Vietnam and I gave her the short version. She became emotional and started to tear up and then she actually thanked me for being in her country and helping her people.

That was the first time I had ever been thanked for being in Vietnam. And it came from a Vietnamese lady who was there as a child and was fortunate enough to have escaped. If you do the math, she was nine years old in 1975. In 1968 she would have been two or three years old. The same time I was in Vietnam. You cannot make this stuff up. Whether you call it fate, or destiny, or simply things happening for a reason, there was no doubt in my mind that this had to be a sign, and a good one at that. And all this only happened because I changed flights and ended up next to her on a plane from Dallas. I gave the woman my business card, and I honestly expect to hear from her again someday.

I think about this experience quite often. Overall it was both sobering and extremely moving. I look at that chance encounter and think that maybe, just maybe, in a strange way, some of those people were helped because of our involvement in Vietnam. Even though they had to escape and run for their lives, maybe we held off the inevitable long enough to make their freedom possible. I had never looked at it that way before because I had never spoken to anyone who experienced it in person until that moment. And her thanking me, truly thanking me, for my service, was a sweet reward so long in coming, but also so very, very gratifying in the end.

Appendix I

Motor Sports History

1987–1988

- One of two principals in signing, to a multi-year agreement, Toyota Motor Sales USA as the sole engine manufacturer for the Formula Atlantic Championship (renamed the Toyota Atlantic Championship). Subsequently assisted in acquiring Yokohama Tires USA as the sole tire supplier for the Toyota Atlantic Championship and ESPN Speed Week for national television coverage of the series.

1989

- Series Administrator Toyota Atlantic Championship–Pacific Division.
- Negotiated contract with FISA (Fédération Internationale du Sport Automobile) for the Formula Atlantic Championship (Pacific Division) as the sole professional support race for the United States Formula One Grand Prix/Phoenix.
- Named Pro Road Racing Coordinator for Seattle International raceway.

1991

- Assisted in production of the richest ever Formula Atlantic Race at Road America ($100,000), Elkhart Lake, WI.

1992

- Technical Administrator for the SCCA American Continental Championship.
- Contingency Sponsorship Coordinator of the SCCA Toyota Atlantic Championship.
- Contingency Sponsorship Coordinator SCCA Oldsmobile Pro Series.

- Contingency Sponsorship Coordinator SCCA American Continental Championship.

1985–1992

Assisted with event management, organization, technical administration, and/or scheduling of professional racing series at the following race circuits:

- Firebird Raceway (Chandler, AZ)
- Heartland Park (Topeka, KS)
- Laguna Seca Raceway (Monterey, CA)
- Memphis Motorsports Park (Memphis, TN)
- Mid-Ohio Sports Car Course (Lexington, OH)
- Portland International Raceway (Portland, OR)
- Race City Speedway (Calgary, Alberta, Canada)
- Road America (Elkhart Lake, WI)
- Road Atlanta (Atlanta/Chamblee, GA)
- Sears Point (Infineon) International Raceway (Sonoma, CA)
- Seattle International Raceway (Kent, WA)
- Watkins Glen International Raceway (Watkins Glen, NY)
- Willow Springs Raceway (Lancaster, CA)
- Westwood Motorsports Park (Vancouver, BC, Canada)

Assisted with event management, organization, technical administration, and/or scheduling of professional racing series at the following temporary race circuits:

- Des Moines, IA
- Long Beach, CA
- Miami, FL
- Montreal (Quebec, Canada)
- St. Petersburg, FL
- Spokane, WA
- Tacoma, WA
- Trois Rivières (Quebec, Canada)
- Vancouver (British Columbia, Canada)

1993–2012

- Facility manager for Robin Automotive, Inc., (Vintage & Historic Race Car Restoration shop) (Sears Point Raceway) Sonoma, California.
- Owner, Fortner Motorsports, motor sports consulting firm and vintage/historic restoration company.

Appendix II

Vintage/Historic Race History Results

4th Place

1996 Monterey Historics—Monterey, California
Formula One
McLaren M19A—Chris MacAllister, Indianapolis, Indiana

2nd Place

1997 Wine Country Classic—Sonoma, California
Formula One
March 811—Chris Bender, Reno, Nevada

1st Place

1997 Monterey Historics—Monterey, California
Formula One
March 811—Chris Bender, Reno, Nevada

1st Place

1997 Portland Historics—Portland, Oregon
Formula One
March 811—Chris Bender, Reno, Nevada

1st Place

1997 Los Angeles Grand Prix—Los Angeles, California
Formula One
March 811—Chris Bender, Reno, Nevada

1st Place

2000 Coronado Naval Air Station Speed Festival—Coronado, California

CanAm
McLaren M6B—Peter Stoneberg, Tiburon, California

4th Place

2001 Sears Point Raceway Classic—Sonoma, California
Formula One
Ferrari 312 T2—Chris MacAllister, Indianapolis, Indiana

1st Place

2001 CSRG Fall Classic—Sears Point Raceway, Sonoma, California
Formula One
Alfa Romeo 179B—Peter Stoneberg, Tiburon, California

1st Place

2001 Monterey Historics—Monterey, California
Formula One
Ferrari 312 T2—Chris MacAllister, Indianapolis, Indiana

1st Place

2001 Monterey Historics—Monterey, California
FIA Sports Cars
Gulf Mirage GR7—Chris MacAllister, Indianapolis, Indiana

1st Place

2003 Kohler Brian Redman Classic—Elkhart Lake, Wisconsin
CanAm
McLaren M8FP—Dino Crescentini, Malibu, California

2nd Place

2004 Kohler Brian Redman Classic—Elkhart Lake, Wisconsin
CanAm
McLaren M8FP—Dino Crescentini, Malibu, California

2nd Place

2004 Circuit Gilles Villenueve—Montreal, Quebec, Canada
Formula One
McLaren M19A—Dino Crescentini, Malibu, California

2nd Place

2004 Monterey Historics—Monterey, California

Vintage/Historic Race History Results

FIA Sports Cars
Lister Jaguar—John Mozart, Palo Alto, California

1st Place

2004 Monterey Historics—Monterey, California
CanAm
McLaren M6—Steve Cook, Yountville, California

2nd Place

2006 Wine Country Classic—Sears Point Raceway, Sonoma, California
FIA Sports Cars/2 liter
Lotus 23—Peter Stoneberg, Tiburon, California

1st Place

2006 Kohler Classic Grand Prix—Elkhart Lake, Wisconsin
CanAm
McLaren M8F—Wade Carter, Seattle, Washington

1st Place

2009 Monterey Historics—Monterey, California
CanAm
Lola T310—Bobby Rahal, New Albany, Ohio

1st Place

2009 Historic Grand Prix—Sears Point Raceway, Sonoma, California
Formula One
March 821—Chris Bender, Reno, Nevada

1st Place

2010 Circuit Mt. Tremblant Historic Grand Prix—St. Jovite, Quebec, Canada
Formula One
March 821—Chris Bender, Reno, Nevada

1st Place

2010 Historic Grand Prix, Barber Motorsports Park—Birmingham, Alabama
Formula One
March 821—Chris Bender, Reno, Nevada

1st Place

2011 Circuit Mt. Tremblant Historic Grand Prix—St. Jovite, Quebec, Canada

Formula One
March 821—Chris Bender, Reno, Nevada

1st Place

Historic Grand Prix—Road America, Elkhart Lake, Wisconsin
Formula One
March 821—Chris Bender, Reno, Nevada

1st Place

2011 Monterey Historics—Monterey, California
CanAm
McLaren M8F—Wade Carter, Seattle, Washington

1st Place

2011 Monterey Historics—Monterey, California
Formula One
March 821—Chris Bender, Reno, Nevada

1st Place

2011 Historic Grand Prix—Infineon Raceway, Sonoma, California
Formula One
March 821—Chris Bender, Reno, Nevada

Appendix III

Statistics from the Vietnam War

(taken from *Vietnam War Facts, Stats and Myths*, https://www.uswings.com/about-us-wings/vietnam-war-facts/)

Totals

9,087,000 military personnel served on active duty during the official Vietnam era (August 5, 1964, to May 7, 1975).
2,709,918 Americans served in uniform in Vietnam.
240 men were awarded the Medal of Honor during the Vietnam War.

Of Those Lost

The first man to die in Vietnam was James Davis in 1961. He was with the 509th Radio Research Station. The Davis Station in Saigon was named for him.
Five men killed in Vietnam were only 16 years old.
The oldest man killed was 62 years old.
58,148 were killed in Vietnam, 75,000 were severely disabled, and of those 23,214 were 100 percent disabled, 5,283 lost limbs and 1,081 sustained multiple amputations.
Of those killed, 61 percent were younger than 21 years old.
11,465 of those killed were younger than 20 years old.
Of those killed, 17,539 were married.
The average age of the men killed: 23.1 years.
87 percent of Americans hold Vietnam Veterans in high esteem.
There is no difference in drug usage between Vietnam Veterans and non–Vietnam Veterans of the same age group (Source: Veterans Administration Study).
Vietnam Veterans are less likely to be in prison—only one-half of 1 percent of Vietnam Veterans have been jailed for crimes.

85 percent of Vietnam Veterans made successful transitions to civilian life.
97 percent of Vietnam Veterans were honorably discharged.
91 percent of Vietnam Veterans say they are glad they served.
74 percent say they would serve again, even knowing the outcome.

Many Still Missing

As of April 14, 2017, there are 1,611 Americans still unaccounted for from the Vietnam War across Vietnam (1,258), Laos (297), Cambodia (49), and China (7).

The sacrifice of every veteran of the Vietnam War
should count for something.
Don't forget them.

Appendix IV

HMM 262 Operations, 1968–1969

Operations—Start Date—End Date

Operation Kentucky: 1 November 1967–28 February 1969*
Operation Scotland II: 15 April 1968–28 February 1969*
Operation Napoleon/Saline: 20 January 1968–9 December 1968*
Operation Nevada Eagle: 17 May 1968–28 February 1969*

Sketch of a CH-46D Sea Knight commissioned by Tim and drawn by Orlando "Lonnie" Ortega in 2018 (http://www.lonnieortegaaviationart.com/).

HMM 262 Operations, 1968–1969

Operation Dawson River: 28 November 1968–26 January 1969**
Operation Marshall Mountain: 9 December 1968–28 February 1969*
Operation Taylor Canyon: 6 December 1968–8 Marchy 1969*
Operation Fayette Canyon: 15 December 1968–8 March 1969*
Operation Baxter Garden: 10 April 1968–Unknown***
Operation Dawson River West: 2 January 1969–12 January 1969**
Operation Dawson River South (renamed Dewey Canyon):
    22 January 1969–18 March 1969*
Operation Dewey Canyon: 22 January 1969–19 March 1969*
Operation Purple Martin: 15 March–2 May 1969*
Operation Montana Mauler: 23 March 1969–3 April 1969***
Operation Virginia Ridge: 30 April 1969–16 July 1969***
Operation Apache Snow: 10 May 1969–7 June 1969***
Operation Cameron Falls: 29 May 1969–23 June 1969***
Operation Utah Mesa: 11 June 1969–9 July 1969***
Operation Iroquois Grove: 15 June 1969–25 September 1969 (Unknown)
Operation Arlington Canyon: 3 July 1969–21 September 1969++
Operation Idaho Canyon: 23 July 1969–25 September 1969++

  * Wikipedia.org—Vietnam War Operations
  ** Headquarters Company 9th Marine Regiment 3rd Marine Division records
  *** 2nd Battalion, 5th Marines documents
  ++ Texas Tech University Vietnam Center & Sam Johnson Vietnam Archive

(NOTE: Other operations, information, and dates can be found here)

Appendix V

Timothy R. Fortner: Citations and Awards

National Defense Service Medal

Vietnamese Service Medal w/2 Stars

Vietnamese Campaign Medal

Republic of Vietnam Cross of Gallantry w/Palm

Air Medal w/Bronze Star for 1st Strike Flight Award

Air Medal Strike Flight Awards w/Numeral 24 for 24 Strike Flights

Good Conduct Medal

Combat Air Crew Wings w/3 Stars

Meritorious Mast

Honorable Discharge

Appendix VI

Timothy R. Fortner: Military Affiliations

Lifetime Member USMC Combat Air Crew Association
Lifetime Member VFW—Veterans of Foreign Wars
Lifetime Member Vietnam Veterans of America
Lifetime Member Disabled American Veterans
Lifetime Member "Marines—Together We Served"

Glossary

A-4: Attack jet "Skyhawk"

AFVN: Armed Forces Vietnam. Military television and radio station broadcasting to troops from in-country

Air America: Arguably, the airline owned by the CIA

AK-47: Russian automatic rifle

APU: Auxiliary Power Unit

Arty: Artillery

C-4: Plastic, putty, textured explosive carried by infantry soldiers. It burns like Sterno when lit, and was used to heat C-rations in the field.

C-47: Twin-engine transport/cargo plane "Skytrain" or "Dakota" (Douglas DC-3)

C-123: Twin-engine transport/cargo plane "Provider"

C-130: Large four-engine prop cargo/transport plane "Hercules"

Cattle cars: Slang for military buses

Charlie Med or "C Med": Medical Battalion Hospital

Chicom: Chinese Communist

Claymore: A command-detonated, directional anti-personnel mine

CONUS: Continental United States

DMZ: Demilitarized Zone

Dzus button: One-quarter-turn fastening device

F-4: Attack jet/fighter jet "Phantom"

FAC: Forward Air Controller

Frag/Fragging: Tossing a hand grenade at or shooting an unpopular superior NCO or officer—normally because he was about to get you killed because he was stupid, in retaliation for a wrongdoing.

Glossary

Gooks: A derogatory slang term for Southeast Asians

HE: High Explosive

HMM: Helicopter Marine Medium

Hootch: A structure consisting of a wood frame, peaked roof, open areas for "windows," and a raised floor.

IFR: Instrument Flight Rules

Incendiary: Bullets or rounds that are used to set the target on fire

Klick: Kilometer

LPH: Landing Platform Amphibious

LZ: Landing Zone

MAG: Marine Aircraft Group

Marston matting: Ribbed steel planks that hook together to form a flat, solid decking. Used for temporary runways.

MAW: Marine Aircraft Wing

MP: Military Police (normally Army)

MPC: Military Payment Certificate or "Scrip" (money)

Mule: Aircraft tow vehicle

NCOIC: Non-Commissioned Officer in Charge

NVA: North Vietnamese Army (regular army)

OIC: Officer in Charge

OV-10: Attack and observation turbo-prop aircraft "Bronco"

Piss tube: Six-inch-diameter tube sunk in the dirt/sand for pissing into

PMAG: Provisional Marine Aircraft Group

PT: Physical Training

QC: Quality Control: A check to ensure work was performed correctly

RADALT: Radar Altimeter

REMF: Rear Echelon Mother Fucker. Term used to describe office people to the rear of the fighting.

RTB: Return to Base

S-2: Intelligence section

Salt: Guy who had been around a long time compared to others

Short-timer: Guy who had only a little time left in country

SAS: Stability Augmentation System, sort of an autopilot

Semper Fi: Short for Semper Fidelis (Latin). The Marine Corps motto meaning "Always Faithful."

SKS: Short for "Samozarydnyj Karabin sistemy Simonova," a Soviet semi-automatic carbine rifle

Sky crane: Large Sikorsky helicopter used for lifting very heavy loads

SP: Shore Patrol (normally Navy)

TACAN: Tactical Air Navigation unit

TDY: Temporary Assigned Duty/Temporary duty

Tracers: Bullets with coating on nose that burns brightly to show bullets' trajectory

West Pac: Western Pacific Theater of Operations

VA: U.S. Department of Veterans Affairs

VC/Victor Charlie—Viet Cong: Political organization and army. Guerrilla and regular army units. Organized and highly effective.

VERTOL: Vertical Takeoff and Landing division of Boeing

VMO: Marine Observation Squadron

Water buffalo: Local buffalo with big horns

Water buffalo: Water tank on wheels

Yellow sheet: Form filled out by pilots explaining problems with aircraft systems

Index

Numbers in **_bold italics_** indicate pages with illustrations

Air California (Air Cal) 37–39
Anheuser-Busch 81
Aptos, California 19
Armed Forces Vietnam (AFVN) 75
Aviation Crash and Rescue School 36–37
aviation guarantee program 36

Bahnhof, Mary 167–171
Ballard, Mike 113–115
Bangkok, Thailand 112
USS *Bear* 133, 135
Berman, Dr. Peter 163–165, 172–174
USS *Bexar* 133
Biloxi, Mississippi 84
Boeing CH-46D Sea Knight helicopter 42–43, 45, 47, **_51_**, 53, 56, 59, 63, 72, 79, 84, 95, 110–111, 115, 133, 168
Boeing VERTOL (VERtical Take Off and Landing) 99
Browning .50-caliber machine gun (fifty-cal or .50-cal) 45–46, 48, 50, 52, 90, 92, 97–98, 108, **_113_**, 116
Budweiser beer 80–81, 85
bullet bouncer 46, 50, 56, 63, 90, 161
Burr, Mr. (Santa Cruz High School principal) 9, 14–16, 18

C4 (plastic explosive) 90
Cabrillo Junior College 19
Cam Lo 94, 116
Camp Carroll 52, 54–55, 65, 69, 94, 168
Camp Pendleton 35, 137–138, 140
The Cardinal (Santa Cruz High School yearbook) 12–14
Carling Black Label beer 78, 119, 121
CH-47 Chinook helicopter 80–81
Chu Lai Air Base 119, 121–124, **_146_**, 152
Cobra gunship 94
Cowells Beach 8
Cua Viet River 68

Danang, Vietnam 42–43, 58–59, 78, 84–85, 112–113, 115, 119, 130–132, 137–**_138_**, 178; Harbor 134

Davey Jones' Locker 114
Demilitarized Zone 43, 128
Disabled American Veterans (DAV) 175
Dobson, George H. (Director of the Monterey County Military & Veterans Affairs Office) 175
Dong Ha, Vietnam 68, 128

El Toro MCAS 39–40
ET 8 (Echo Tango) 50, 56–58

F-4 Phantom 69, 94–95, 97, 109, 123
F-18 Super Hornet 66
Fire Base Alpha 168
Fonda, Jane 139
Force Recon 47–48
Fresno, California 39

GE T58-10 turbo shaft engine 56–57
Guam 179
guard duty 100–103

Hamburg, Germany 90
Hanoi, Vietnam 139, 178
Hawaii 112–114, 150, 158, 161
HMM 161 80, 96, 104, 125
HMM 262 42–43, 50, 57–58, 69, 76–78, 86, 96, 98, 103–105, **_107_**, 125, 130, 132
HMMT (Helicopter Marine Medium Training) 302 37–38, 42
Hong Kong 112
Honolulu, Hawaii 42, 114–115, 158
Hue, Vietnam 98

infantry training regiment (ITR) 35
USS *Iwo Jima* **_131_**, 133, 134, **_138_**

Jacksonville, Florida 37
John Wayne 90
Jolly Green Giants (rescue helicopter) 61, 84–86, 89

Karwatowicz, Dr. Adam 171, 175

Index

LA Dodgers 154
Las Vegas Strip 148
Lemore NAS (Naval Air Station) 40
Lindbergh Field 35
Lockheed Electra Turbo Prop 38
LZ Argonne **89**

Mach 1 Mustang 83, 147
MAG 39 (Marine Air Group) 76–77, 100
Marble Mountain Air Facility (MMAF) 130
Marina del Rey, California 148, 150
Marine Air Detachment, Naval Air Station, Naval Aviation Technical Training Center Jacksonville, Florida (MADNASNATTC-JAX) 37
Marston Matting 57, 100
MCAS (Marine Corps Air Station) Yuma 141
McMann, Dr. 170–171, 175
Mineral Wells, Texas 99
Monterey, California 38, 124, 169, 175
Monterey County Veterans Affairs Office 162
MOS (military occupation specialty) 36, 158
MPC (military payment certificates) 82

National Vietnam War Museum 99
Naval Air Station Memphis 37
Naval Air Station Patuxent River 37
Naval Base San Diego 137
NVA (North Vietnamese Army) 48, 69, 73, 94, 97–98, 106, 110–111, 116–117, 127–128

Ocean Tennis Courts 148, 150–151
Okinawa, Japan 42, 85, 113, 115, 135, 179
Operation "Lancaster II" **93**
Orange County airport 37–38
Outrigger Hotel 114, 150
OV-10 125

Pacheco Pass 39–40
Palm Springs, California 148
Palo Alto, California 163
the Philippines 112
Phu Bai, Vietnam 130–132
Pleen, G/Sgt. 86–87, 165
Portland International Raceway 158
PTSD 59, 160, 162–164, 166–173, 176–178; diagnosis of 164–165

Quang Tri, Vietnam **43**, 46, 52, 55, 63, 65, 69, 72, **75**, 78, **79**, **83**–85, 89, 92, 94, 96, 98, 100, **101**, 103, 110, 115, 121, 124–125, 160, 168; arrival 42; C-Med, Charlie Med (medical unit) 49, 68–69, 109, 115, 129, 169; departure from 130–132; enlisted club 74; flight line 90; handball court 104–105; PX 83; "shitters" 80; "Steak" 74

Rahway, New Jersey 157
Rambo 96

USS *Repose* 49, 169
Rockpile 55, 61, **66**, 71, 73, 106, 116, 168
Route 9 117
Rusty (Tim's best friend) 9–12, 18–24, 34, 36–37, 84–85, 88–**89**, 91–92, **120**, **146**; death 152; downward spiral 150–152; R&R visit to 119–124

Saigon, Vietnam 119, 178–179
Salinas, California 21
San Diego, California 137, **138**
San Francisco, California 38, 40, 84, 114, 138–141, 178
San Francisco Giants 154
San Jose, California 38–39, 149, 150
USS *Sanctuary* 49, 63, 71–72, 85, 109–111, 169
Santa Ana, California 37–39, 41–42, 84
Santa Claus 88
Santa Cruz, California 7, 9, 17, 34, 39, 85, 114, 146, 149, 150, 153, 157, 158, 176; Boardwalk 12, 19; High School 7, 10, 12–13, 16
Santa Monica, California 148, 157
SCCA (Sports Car Club of America) 158
Sears Point Raceway 158
Seaside, California 162
SFO 138, 158, 165
Short Timer's Ribbon 122–123
Shurley, Cpl. Marlon 50–58
Sonoma, California 158, 176
Soquel, California 7; High School 7, 9
Southwest Airlines 178
SSgt. Segovia 38–40
Steamer Lane 7
Sunshine Tennis Courts 158

TACAN (TAC-tical Air Navigation) 80
Texas Tech University 178
Thach Han River 78, 102, 125
Thailand 85
The Tiger Bar & Grille 74–**75**, 76–78, **79**, 81, 83, 85–86, 89, 92; construction of 75; success of 76
Tokyo, Japan 112
Travis AFB (Air Force Base) 42
Trigalet, Lt. Robert 104–105

United States Air Force 77, 84–86; attempt to enlist 21
United States Army 78–81, 85
United States Marine Corps (USMC) 85; boot camp 22, 24–36; enlistment 21–22; enlistment pledge 5; R&R policy 89; Recruit Depot (MCRD) 25, 32–35
United States Navy 78–80, 135; attempt to enlist 21; R&R Welcoming Center 114

VA 162–164, 166, 169, 170, 172, 175; disability benefit 173, 174, 176
VA Palo Alto medical facility 163, 167, 171, 173, 175

Vandegrift Combat Base *43*, 93–94, 96, 105, 115, 117, 128
Vernon, Sergeant (truant officer) 9–10, 14–16
Viet Cong (VC) 44, 47–48, 69, 94, 98, 106–107, 117, 127–129
Vietnamization Plan 130, 139
Villareal, Manuel 142–144
VMO-6 125
Vung Tau, Vietnam 119

Waikiki Beach, Hawaii 150

Wallace, Cpl. Mick 87
Waters, Tom 84–86, 89
Woodlawn Cemetery 154
World War II 90, 168

Yuma, Arizona 144

Zeigler, William (Veterans Affairs Service Officer) 162–163

www.ingramcontent.com/pod-product-compliance
Ingram Content Group UK Ltd.
Pitfield, Milton Keynes, MK11 3LW, UK
UKHW042007140426
5217IPUK00015B/1035